Aspies
on
Mental
Health

in the same series

Asperger Syndrome and Employment
Edited by Genevieve Edmonds and Luke Beardon
ISBN 978 1 84310 648 7

Asperger Syndrome and Social Relationships
Edited by Genevieve Edmonds and Luke Beardon
ISBN 978 1 84310 647 0

of related interest

Mental Health Aspects of Autism and Asperger Syndrome
Mohammad Ghaziuddin
ISBN 978 1 84310 727 9 (paperback)
ISBN 978 1 84310 733 0 (hardback)

Aspies
on
Mental
Health

Speaking
for Ourselves

Edited by Luke Beardon and Dean Worton

Jessica Kingsley *Publishers*
London and Philadelphia

First published in 2011
by Jessica Kingsley Publishers
116 Pentonville Road
London N1 9JB, UK
and
400 Market Street, Suite 400
Philadelphia, PA 19106, USA

www.jkp.com

Library of Congress Cataloging in Publication Data
Aspies on mental health : speaking for ourselves / [edited by] Luke Beardon and Dean
Worton.
      p. ; cm.
   ISBN 978-1-84905-152-1 (alk. paper)
   1. Asperger's syndrome--Patients--Biography. I. Beardon, Luke. II. Worton, Dean.
   [DNLM: 1. Asperger Syndrome--complications--Personal Narratives. 2. Asperger
Syndrome--psychology--Personal Narratives. 3. Adaptation, Psychological--Personal
Narratives. 4. Adult. 5. Mental Health Services--Personal Narratives. 6. Social
Support--Personal Narratives. WM 203.5]
   RC553.A88A797 2011
   616.85'8832--dc22
                              2010041573

British Library Cataloguing in Publication Data
A CIP catalogue record for this book is available from the British Library

ISBN 978 1 84905 152 1

Printed and bound in Great Britain

Contents

Introduction

Luke Beardon

I believe that there is a qualitative difference between mental illness and mental ill health. I also believe that there is no reason to suspect that people with Asperger syndrome (AS) have any more chance of being mentally ill compared to the predominant neurotype (PNT). However, I do believe that there is a significantly higher risk of people with AS developing mental health problems (i.e. mental ill health) compared to the PNT. The difference between mental illness and mental ill health is crucial. My understanding is that mental illness as a primary condition is neurologically based – one is schizophrenic, for example, as a direct result of neurological issues. However, I would argue that mental ill health as a secondary psychiatric condition is very much environmentally influenced – that is to say that the individual develops mental health conditions as a result of environmental factors rather than directly neurological ones. It is the brain that is affected, not the brain that is 'at fault'. So, in brief, one is mentally ill if one's brain is not working as it should; one develops mental ill health when environmental factors influence the brain to such a degree that it becomes poorly. If this is the case, and I see no reason why it does not stand up as an argument, then the statistics that suggest that people with AS are more likely to develop mental ill health (as opposed to being primarily mentally ill) mean that it is the environment that is causing such a major problem compared to the PNT who are not affected in the same way. As an equation this hypothesis could be summed up thus:

$$AS + environment = higher\ chance\ of\ mental\ ill\ health$$

Now, we can agree (surely) that there is no way that an individual's AS can be 'changed' in any way – nor would we want to do this. Thus, if people with AS are to suffer less frequently, with less severity, and with better outcomes from mental ill health, then it makes perfect sense to suggest that the *environment* needs changing in the equation – *not the person with AS*. It simply is not possible to influence the individual's AS (though, of course it is possible to change how the individual exists as a person with AS), but it *is* perfectly possible to influence the environment.

PNT influence on mental health

Are people with AS often loners, excluding themselves from society and seeking solitude because of the nature of AS? Or is it because the environment around them is so alien, so distressingly chaotic and unreasonable, that a choice between 'joining in' and exclusion is practically a moot one? It is the PNT world that people with AS are expected to 'fit into' and environmentally, in the main, it is the PNT way of doing things and existing that is expected. Is it any wonder, then, that the person with AS can end up with severe mental ill health? The most basic principle and yet one which has yet to be fundamentally embedded in the psyche of most PNTs is this:

> **Forcing individuals with AS to exist in a PNT world without making any changes, can be (and often is) extremely detrimental to the mental well-being of the person with AS.**

Whilst this is (deliberately) a generalisation, there is enough evidence, I would suggest, to support this statement fully. From a personal perspective not a day goes by (excepting holidays, etc.) when I am not in contact with a situation demonstrating the devastating affect the PNT way of doing things has on a person with AS. And yet, time after time after time I meet people who are essentially told by 'professionals' that the fault is theirs, and they are the ones who need to change and adapt to the situation, and they are the ones who should take the responsibility to make those adaptations (almost always with no appropriate support). Surely, aside from the ineffectual aspect of following this pathway, it is highly unethical in this day and age of 'reasonable adjustment' and so called acceptability of differing neurotypes? While a small proportion of the population (a tiny minority) might understand that adapting the environment is the best way to reduce mental ill health in people with AS, the vast majority – and I include most mental health professionals in this statement – still do not recognise the extreme destructive affect that environmental factors have on people with AS. In addition – which is basically a double whammy hammer blow to fragile mental health – professionals then expect the individual with AS to somehow change themselves to cope with the very factors that are causing the distress. Is this intelligent thinking? Is this professionally ethical? Is it, in any way, appropriate? Is it the way forward in reducing mental ill health in people with AS? I suspect a resounding 'no' is the most applicable answer to each of the questions.

Environmental factors

The following are some of the key environmental factors that need to be taken into account from my point of view:

- diagnosis
- post-diagnostic support
- social environment
- communication
- empathic understanding
- honesty/trust
- sensory environment
- fairness/justice.

DIAGNOSIS

Currently, if we are to believe published epidemiological studies alongside statistical data from local authorities, it would seem that there are a lot of people out there who would qualify for a diagnosis of AS but do not have one. If one has AS but does not know it, then there is potential for major problems with identification of self and understanding of who one is – and why. This is not to suggest that every single person with AS requires a diagnosis, but the opportunity to explore and understand one's self is one which should not be denied anyone. However, as noted, many people remain undiagnosed.

Second, many of the diagnostic processes are potentially going to have a negative affect on an individual's mental health. The very medically based deficit model of AS that is used (based on medical sets of diagnostic criteria) tends to present AS in a very negative light – it is often a question of 'Let's see what's wrong with you' as opposed to 'Let's see whether you are a person with AS'. Simply have a look at most diagnostic criteria to see what I mean. This is unhealthy and, I would argue, unjust; simply because people with AS think differently to those without, does not mean that people with AS are 'in the wrong'. Conversely, I would suggest that the AS way of thinking is often far superior in many ways to the PNT model. Thus, a dramatic change in how people are diagnosed could potentially reduce negative feelings about having AS which can lead to mental ill health.

POST-DIAGNOSTIC SUPPORT
This is a vital area which is almost nationally unavailable as a statutory support mechanism. Good post-diagnostic support is crucial for many people in exploring what the diagnosis means to them. I would go as far as to suggest that the later on in life the diagnosis is made, the more critical good post-diagnostic support becomes. The lack of support can lead to all sorts of problems for the individual, who is usually left to his/her own devices – and, thus, often at the mercy of the internet, which may not provide the most appropriate information specific to that individual. As with all things related to AS, the support required is very individual, being dependent on a variety of factors. No support, or the wrong support, following a diagnosis, is potentially of high consequence in the individual's mental well-being. Getting it right, on the other hand, could go a long way to reducing potential mental health issues.

SOCIAL ENVIRONMENT

Consider the following: A member of public, on seeing someone behaving in a slightly socially odd way, is deemed perfectly reasonable to ignore the person and get on with their lives as though nothing has happened. A person with AS, faced with everyone around them behaving in what they see as a highly socially odd way is expected to fit in and embrace the oddness as though it were perfectly natural. When the person with AS sensibly either ignores the behaviour or tries to encourage what they regard as appropriate (AS) social behaviour they are then ostracised and deemed 'in the wrong' – what double standards are these?

The PNT social environment for a person with AS can be one of the most chaotic and baffling environments to be in; quietly avoiding interaction with this strange breed, however commonsensical it may be, is not accepted by the PNT. People with AS are expected and encouraged to accept what they may regard as aberrant behaviour, much to the detriment of their mental well-being.

There *must* be a move towards harmonious co-existence in the social world if people with AS are not to be (a) excluded from society as a result of not coping with the PNT social expectations, and (b) forced into mental ill health as a result of having to force themselves to adapt their own social behaviour simply to suit the PNT.

COMMUNICATION

At some point the PNT should recognise that the use of language (perhaps I should say misuse of language) can have a severe and lasting effect on people with AS. From annoying tautological language to blatant lies, people with AS are faced with a barrage of inaccurate and misleading communications which they are expected to translate and deal with. This can lead to all sorts of problematic encounters for people with AS and – as can be expected – can lead to stress, anxiety, and depression. Relatively simple changes in accuracy of language by those around them can make an enormous difference to people with AS. However, until the PNT realise the negative impact and extensive repercussions that their form of communication has on those with AS it is likely that continued stress for people with AS will be the norm.

EMPATHIC UNDERSTANDING

We are often told that people with AS lack empathy; while this might be the case when assessing empathic understanding across neurological boundaries (i.e. empathy towards those without AS) it would be inaccurate to suggest that a total lack of empathy is evident for all people with AS. However, when attempting to find good empathic processing within the PNT in relation to those with AS it is almost impossible. There is almost no empathic understanding within the PNT of those with AS. This means that the majority of the PNT simply do not understand nor empathise with those with AS.

If people with AS are to be supported to reduce issues of mental ill health, then those around them must learn to understand and accept how different the perspectives of those with AS are – in addition to accepting that those differing perspectives are just as valid (if not more so) than their own. This, it appears to me, is problematic for many of the PNT – and, thus, the problem is laid firmly back at the door of the individual with AS. This lack of flexibility of thought within the PNT population has dangerous consequences for the person with AS.

HONESTY/TRUST

Everyone feels better when they are surrounded by people who they feel they can trust and who will be honest when required. There is a correlation between feelings of contentment in a relationship and levels of mutual honesty and trust. However, very often the experience of the person with AS is that people are not to be trusted, nor is everyone (anyone?) honest to the degree required for simple levels of contentment. How is one supposed to feel content with a world that lies on a daily basis, that deceives (deliberately or otherwise), and lets down with regular and frequent occurrence? Moreover, how is one supposed to learn who is trustworthy and honest compared to someone who is not?

Ensuring that those in contact with a person with AS develop their levels of ability to be honest and trustworthy is, I think, one of the most important ways of supporting individuals. What may seem less than relevant to the PNT can be of utmost importance to the person with AS; slight changes to ways of communicating and behaving can make extraordinary differences to the person with AS.

SENSORY ENVIRONMENT

It is well known that the sensory environment is often perceived very differently by the person with AS, and yet it is unlikely that sensory issues within the environment are usually taken into account. The distress that sensory issues can cause to an individual is immense; simply accepting this as fact can go a long way towards the paradigm shift in understanding that the PNT need to embrace if people with AS are not to be forced down the path of mental ill health.

The scale of the impact of the sensory environment should be at the forefront of anyone who is involved with a person with AS. Changes to the physical environment may be of paramount importance if the individual is expected to survive with emotional and mental well-being intact.

FAIRNESS/JUSTICE

This is an area that is not often cited as being related to AS; however, I feel that it is one that can cause immeasurable mental distress to many individuals, and is worthy of note. Many people with AS appear to have an extremely well-developed and honed sense of right and wrong – especially when it comes to the fair treatment of people. Living in a world that is often unfair and unjust, therefore, can have a detrimental affect on the individual, sometimes to the point of causing secondary psychiatric conditions such as depression.

It is clearly not possible for this element of the environment to be changed overnight; global injustice is likely to continue for a long time yet. However, it is important to recognise that on a day-to-day basis the individual with AS is likely to react more strongly to perceived injustices that surround them compared to many others.

Summary of thoughts

This book will probably make you cry. It is full of heartbreaking real-life events that in many ways should never have occurred. It is also a testament to the extraordinary people who have written the accounts. I am deeply privileged to know many of the authors, and others who could recount similar tales. The very real fact is that this book should not have had to be written. The very real fact is that it has been. And the very real fact is that the world is a long way off from ensuring that environmentally led mental ill health is a thing of the past for people with AS.

What is clear within the pages of this book is the power that the PNT have over many people with AS, in particular the 'professionals' – and, even more in particular, mental health professionals. There are doubtless some good professionals out there in terms of understanding AS, though I would suggest that they are very much in the minority. Similarly, in the general population there are some exceptional individuals belonging to the PNT who have a positive impact on the lives of people with AS. However, until there is a far greater understanding of AS and how the environment (especially the people within it) can and does influence people with AS, and until there are changes made in light of this, people with AS will continue to be vulnerable to mental ill health.

Please – read this book and take it seriously. Then give it to someone else who might make use of it, be it a psychiatrist or a member of a family. It is a must read – for everyone.

Finally, please allow me to introduce some writing that sums up feelings of mental health in a way that few in the world are able to. This is written by *mi amigo* Alex (see Chapter 9) and flies in the face of all those ignorant people who believe that those with AS lack feeling, are poor communicators, and lack creativity. A stunning piece of writing, and one that should never, ever, have had to be written.

Crushed

Trapped between two walls,
There's nowhere for me to go.
As I feel them closing in,
My lungs constrict,
The air becoming thin.

I hold on to the thought,
That surely it must pass.
Overwhelmed by sadness,
Despair envelops me,
Leaving me lifeless, useless.

Descending around me like a mist,
It obscures my vision, distorts my view.
Hazy shadows form, disfiguredly shaped,
Despondency lingers,
Around my shoulders draped.

But that's only the beginning,
The sharp knife plunges in;
Electricity surging through my brain.
Daggers stabbing, piercing,
Intensify the pain.

Only bad feelings,
Only sad thoughts,
Exist in my mind.
Melancholy, alone
In my misery I find.

I need to break through
This curtain, this veil.
Impenetrable, suffocating, until I succumb,
It smothers my life force;
Rendering me frozen, derelict, numb.

Darkness surrounds me,
I will it to come.
Could unconsciousness follow?
Relieve me from this torture;
Overpowered by anguish and sorrow.

Entrapped within the confines of my mind;
I watch, I wait,
Observing, wishing, hoping;
That if and when I am released, I make some sense of the world
around me;
Surviving, coping.

Alex Brown

Chapter 1

Mental Health Services and Me: What Worked, and What Didn't

Janet Christmas

Introduction by Luke Beardon

Janet writes eloquently about her experiences, and one thing in particular struck me as of utmost importance to consider: the very different way in which support strategies might be experienced. It is clear from Janet's writing that 'traditional' ways of support within psychiatric care were of very little use, and in some cases caused further distress. However, alternative therapeutic provision (e.g. knitting in Janet's example) was of great benefit. It underlines the immense importance of treating the individual as a person with AS, rather than simplistically 'treating' a mental illness — there is a huge distinction, conceptually and pragmatically, between the two.

I would argue that all psychiatric units should have AS-specific training as part of their statutory training; the distress caused by lack of understanding of people with AS who have had the misfortune to find themselves in a psychiatric unit can be huge. The potential to cause irreversible mental damage is high. At the very least, all those concerned with psychiatric care should have the opportunity to read and digest Appendix 2 of Janet's writing, which is a wonderful synopsis of various aspects that might influence a person with AS who finds themselves in a unit.

Setting the scene

The first crash came in 1984 and I had no idea what had hit me. It was three in the morning, I was on an oil platform in the middle of the North Sea, and they had just started top-hole drilling; the computer was in bits on the laboratory floor, the company man was screaming at me on the phone because there was no data on his screen. I just 'lost it' and went into some sort of catatonic/hysterical state, blurting out crazy religious statements and fragments of an engineering formula (to predict blow-outs from drilling rate) which I had recently designed and had programmed using Fortran into the computer. In hindsight, I suspect that this was a sort of autistic meltdown, but no one knew anything about this back in 1984.

I must point out that to this day, I have never had a formal autistic spectrum diagnosis. However, even before my first breakdown, I had always known I was 'different', but was not sure why. I always had (and still have) abnormal difficulties with the following:

- inter-personal relationships, especially with colleagues at work
- hypersensitivity to sudden strange noises/smells/visually disturbing patterns
- odd way of dress – must wear natural fabrics
- balance and co-ordination
- eye contact
- face recognition
- social awkwardness and shyness
- panic attacks – especially in supermarkets
- inability to tell the difference between 'left' and 'right'
- obsessions with routine and detail
- working out what people are really thinking (the 'hidden agendas')
- recognition of, and appropriately responding to irony and sarcasm.

As a child I was always getting into trouble from my grandparents for my non-imaginative play (lining up my plastic farm animals in rows, smallest at the left, or repeatedly spinning my favourite toy car on its roof until the paint wore off), and I found play time at school to be an excruciatingly awful ordeal. My problems with co-ordination meant that I could never catch a ball, or even throw a ball so that another child could catch it. I could never work out what was going on in 'Tag' games and tried at all times to stand with my back against a warm, safe wall or to hide under my desk so that I would not be forced to join in the 'play'.

But this was the late 1960s, and, because I was intellectually bright and had a haughty, precocious language, the school psychiatrist who saw me did not assign me for education in a specialist school. My intellectual abilities managed to get me through most things, and although school was torture, I finally found my niche at university where I read for two degrees in geology.

As some of my problems and difficulties seem to closely resemble those experienced by people on the high end of the autistic spectrum, I think the following will be relevant to those readers who have an interest in this field.

The first breakdown

Back to 1984. My memory is patchy, but I somehow managed to catch a flight back to Heathrow; however, I caught the wrong train and ended up 120 miles away from home. I must have been home with my parents for about two days, before the GP was called and I found myself in a mental health section of the local hospital. Prior to this admission, I had never had contact with any mental health service.

What follows is not meant to be a criticism of the unit; it must have been very difficult for the staff to have to cope with such a wide range of patients, all with different illnesses and symptoms. At the time of my admission I had no awareness of the problems and issues I have listed at the start of this account, so both nursing staff and I were not in a position to ameliorate my extreme reactions to events as they occurred.

To be honest, I really had no inkling of where I was. I think I imagined I was in some sort of government torture department straight from George Orwell's book, *1984*. I could not forget that it *was* 1984 after all. Then I thought I was back on the rig and that I needed to write down that overpressure formula so that I would not forget it. Other times I thought we were preparing for a nuclear holocaust and decided that the rooms in the hospital with few windows were especially strengthened so that they would serve as a nuclear bunker.

I had no idea who the people were around me, and could not tell who was a nurse, doctor, cleaning staff, patient, or occupational therapist so things rapidly got very complicated. I was totally disorientated and could not work out the geography of the unit and kept struggling to find the safe cold room that I thought was the bunker. An overriding thirst made me compulsively seek out the cold milk machine to drink gallons of the stuff, thereby depriving other patients of their precious supply for tea and coffee.

One patient discovered that setting off the fire alarm would produce an intriguing result (a hysterical screaming fit from me) so she made this a regular source of entertainment. I had been trained in fire-fighting and survival on the rigs, so I would drop to the floor to avoid the ever present fug of cigarette smoke – another source of amusement for staff and patients. The pervasive smell of smoke and the intense heat was a constant difficulty and one nurse had to wrestle with me to prevent me from hurling a metal chair through the window just to get some fresh cool air.

As can be imagined, the other unusual noises (other patients) and smells (disinfectant, strong aftershave/perfume, smoke) in the hospital sent me into orbit and the doctors and staff rapidly lost patience with me. I was shouting, screaming, crying, struggling and upsetting the other patients.

No one could understand what I was shouting about (not surprising really) so, within days of admission, I was subjected to a course of electro-convulsive therapy (ECT). With my memory 'wiped clean' things got even worse. I could not even recognise my parents or my fiancé. In my muddled thinking I concluded that Margaret Thatcher thought I knew too much about the geology of the North Sea and that she and her government were trying to kill me. Each time I was anaesthetised ready for the ECT I reassured myself that this was the execution chamber, and, although I did not really want to die, I told myself that the turmoil would soon be over.

Perhaps if someone had the time to sit down and talk to me, things might have been different. Initially, the services provided by the poor occupational therapists only exacerbated my difficulties. The therapy sessions always started off with a 'music and movement' group with about 40 patients and staff sitting on chairs in a circle within a huge room. Being confronted with so many faces terrified me, and the thought of moving to music brought back awful memories of school dances.

I am someone who, even when well, always avoids 'discos', clubs and dancing. I was once told by a teacher at school that there was more to life than discos so I decided at an early age that I did not need to subject myself such an ordeal. My favourite pastimes are walking by the sea (watching the waves is especially relaxing), collecting postcards, knitting and solving cryptic crosswords.

So the occupational therapy staff would have a struggle to get me to even sit in the room to start with; I surmised they were trying to make me go to a disco against my wishes. And, on the rare occasions when they were successful, I would find myself in difficulties when we were required to throw and catch a soft ball to other people in the circle.

It is a shame that I did not persevere or 'co-operate' with the treatment on offer, as later on in the day things got better when we would be split into smaller groups and assigned to listening to relaxation tapes, craft work, scrabble games, printing or pottery. I responded well to the pottery therapy because it was quiet and because working with my hands stopped the awful sensations churning through my brain. The smell of the wet clay in pottery was lovely and calming, and although I usually fell asleep when listening to the relaxation tapes, at least I was composed and not shouting.

The psychiatrists persistently asking me if I heard 'voices in my head' made no sense to me whatsoever; I have never experienced this phenomenon as I tend to think in pictures and sensations rather than words. My replies to this questioning must have seemed very bizarre.

My medication at the time was 400mg of Largactil, tryptophan and Tryptisol and it was a struggle to remain awake. I was an in-patient at the unit for about three months with another three months of out-patient treatment. As far as I am aware, my diagnosis was a combination of bipolar disorder and clinical depression and the episode was labelled 'nervous breakdown'.

The intervening years

I returned to work, initially at the company library in Aberdeen, then on a land-based oil drilling rig in Spain. But I was fighting constant anxiety and the side effects of the medication all the time. I was sacked after a colleague found me asleep on the night shift.

After getting the sack, I found a job as domestic assistant at a Field Study Centre on the coast of West Wales. This was perfect for me. I had to clean toilets, mop floors, help the chef with catering, make beds and vacuum the guest rooms. I did not mind this at all, as my brain was still numb and it was difficult to make decisions. This was the best occupational therapy I could have had at the time. There was routine and structure to my day. The afternoons were free and I used the time to walk along the coastal paths near the centre on my own, find a good place to sit and simply watch the waves and relax. The environment was so calming that I was able to persuade my GP to reduce my medication. By the end of my stint at the Field Centre, I had weaned myself off all medication.

Unfortunately, the job as a domestic assistant was very poorly paid, and it was not something I could contemplate long term.

I accepted a job offer in the civil service and went to work in London. Still not aware of my difficulties, I ran into more trouble with colleagues in the civil service and with commuting on the noisy tube train. I gradually went downhill again with work-related stress. I stuck with the civil service job for 17 years, with long periods away from work diagnosed variously with stress, depression, post-traumatic stress disorder, and schizophrenia, depending on who was treating me at the time. In 1991, after five years of being free from medication, I was prescribed Seroxat and was given one-to-one counselling. The counselling was not a lot of help. I kept talking about my childhood as I thought that was what was expected of me, hopelessly trying to fathom out why I felt so stressed all the time.

The revelation for me finally came in 1999 when I read a newspaper article about Temple Grandin (a lady in America who has AS). It so accurately reflected my problems that, as I read the article, the hairs on the back of my head stood on end.

Once I was aware of my particular 'triggers' I spoke extensively to my line managers and the 'Welfare at Work' department in an attempt to persuade them to make adjustments that would help me to work effectively. But I was unable to get any support for my requests. My line manager told me that making the adjustments I had requested would 'upset the other members of staff, who could not see anything visibly wrong with me, and therefore would think I was being singled out for unfair special treatment and privileges'. And the very requirements of the job (multitasking, working with constant interruptions in a noisy open-plan office, coping with constant reorganisation and change, communication skills, wearing clothing appropriate for office work) coupled with my particular problems (obsessions with routine and details, face recognition, not being good at socialising/hanging out, workplace bullying) meant that I simply did not fit the bill.

Despite working to the very best of my abilities, I kept getting dismal performance marks, and, as my pay was linked to this, my pay lagged far behind the pay of my colleagues. After a particularly bad crisis in the autumn of 2001, with colleagues harassing me on the phone about work that had not been done to their liking, and a traumatic journey to work, I crashed again with a hysterical screaming fit.

This time I was not admitted as an in-patient. I tried to explain to my psychiatrists that I suspected my underlying problems were possibly due to AS, but they flatly dismissed the suggestion. They told me: 'If you were at all autistic, it would have been diagnosed when you were a child. Children who have autism grow up with autism. As you were not diagnosed as a child, you do not have autism.'

But, my new awareness of my particular issues brought fresh insight for me. I wanted help that was targeted at patients with a diagnosis of AS, but I knew I would not get this. Even as recently as 2001, there were simply no facilities in that part of London for adults with AS. And, without a formal diagnosis, I was at a double disadvantage. Nevertheless I decided to co-operate with whatever was on offer. (Back in 1984, without awareness, I admit that I was arrogant and inflexible. If I thought a particular therapy would not be any good for me, I would not try it and fought with the nurses at every step.)

This time I attended music/movement, creative writing and socialising therapy. All of this helped me to build up my confidence and helped me decide what I was going to do about my life. The music/movement was very scary, but surprisingly I found it helped me to value myself as a person (employment had knocked every ounce of confidence out of my system). The socialising involved such tasks as going to a café with a nurse to learn how to tolerate crowds and noises. I found it helpful to share my irrational fears with everyone in a supportive environment. If these are vocalised, they do not seem so acute, and the therapist can immediately suggest some helpful coping strategies.

Following my therapy I decided that my life could be improved by not trying to live and work in London; I had tried everything and it was simply going to be detrimental to my health to try to go back to my old job. My parents are elderly and they wanted me to move in with them in Norfolk to help care for them and, at the same time, try to rebuild my life.

After the therapy finished, I attended an organisation that helps people build up their confidence enough to start work again following mental illness. Here, in a particularly memorable group therapy session (using a flip chart to list examples) I learnt a lot about assertiveness and just how damaging passive behaviour can be. It was here that I thought I could change my career by learning how to care for elderly people, and, in turn, use that knowledge to learn essential techniques required to care for my father who is coping with the after-effects of a stroke and Parkinson's disease.

So I packed all my belongings and put them in storage and made the move to Norfolk. But, I was still under considerable stress as I had not resigned from work. I thought that, as they had been unable to prevent the bullying and harassment or to make any appropriate adjustments to my working conditions, they had been the cause of my stress and anxiety. I was still hoping that they would be able to find the appropriate niche for me. I had a lot to offer the service with my computing and database skills and it seemed a shame that they could not make use of them. Perhaps they could even consider my working from home in Norfolk.

Meanwhile I had been in touch with Cambridge Lifespan Asperger Syndrome Service (CLASS) – part of the Cambridgeshire and Peterborough Mental Health Partnership NHS and the National

Diagnostic Centre for Adults with Asperger Syndrome. At that time, I thought a diagnosis would help me access social support groups, gain appropriate advice to give to my employers and possibly some social skills training. However, CLASS needed a referral letter from my GP. But, sadly both my GP (now in Norfolk) and my psychiatrist refused to write this letter on the grounds that a diagnosis would be 'irrelevant' or 'not appropriate' in my case.

In an attempt to reduce my anxiety, I decided to take a month's working holiday at a Buddhist community. My job was to clear wild rhododendrons which were colonising the island and overrunning the native woodland plants.

The second breakdown

I had not prepared myself for the amount of social interaction that would be required in such an isolated community, and gradually my stress levels built up. I was in a dormitory of eight people; most of them did not retire until 11 or 12 at night, and they were up again at 04:00 hours for Tara prayers. This, together with the all-night screeching from the oystercatchers on the beach a few yards away meant that I was not getting enough sleep.

Then, two of the people in my working party had to leave for personal reasons and I was the only one left with the rhododendrons. The staff in charge decided it would not be safe for me to work on my own with secateurs and billhooks, and as the rhododendron patch was a good ten-minute walk from the accommodation block they would not be able to render assistance if I had an accident.

So I was assigned a job in the Peace Garden. I thought this would be ideal, but I was deteriorating rapidly and it turned into an unmitigated disaster. Something had 'flipped' in my brain and I was unable to make even simple decisions. The people who managed the Peace Garden needed to go to the mainland for essential supplies, so I was in charge. I was supposed to show visitors around the garden and explain its meaning, and the kitchen staff kept asking me for herbs – such as coriander – that were cultivated in the garden. Although I am a good gardener and normally have an excellent knowledge of plants, my brain seemed to have given up completely. I could not find the coriander and suddenly I realised I could not even tell what was a weed or what was a salad vegetable. I remember thinking that I was dreaming and kept pinching myself to reassure myself that it was a dream and not happening for real. Some visitors arrived and started asking me about the plants. I rushed off in tears and decided to return to the rhododendron patch to try to sleep off whatever it was I was suffering from. But when I walked back to the accommodation block two hours later the deterioration continued and the staff had no other option than to march me (I was struggling and resisted their assistance) to the jetty for the ferry back to hospital.

I freaked when I saw the ambulance waiting for me; memories of the psychiatric unit came flooding back, and I can recall screaming and struggling with the medical staff. I wanted to return to the retreat, not go to a hospital where I thought I would be subjected to ECT. I was assessed and then committed to hospital on a 72-hour Section. I do not remember much about the journey to hospital, but I think there was a lot of shouting and screaming. Again I seemed to be completely disorientated. I thought I was in Swansea (where I had lived for a few years) and when I was on the ferry back to the mainland I thought I was in the cargo hold of an airliner that had been hijacked and we were going to be flown into a large building. I think I was given an injection to sedate me, and my memory of the last part of the journey is hazy.

Strangely enough, within a few minutes of my admission to hospital, I can remember coming to my senses. It quickly dawned on me that I was in a hospital, and, oddly enough, I did not feel afraid. I co-operated with the admission staff, pointing out my tweezers, penknife and other sharp objects that I knew they were obliged to lock away for the safety of patients and staff.

I was put in an observation room next to the nurses' station and left to sleep it off, a bit like sleeping off a hangover. About two days later, when I 'came to' someone gave me a jigsaw puzzle of Culzean Castle to complete. This was the best thing to happen to me at that point, as my brain was too numb to concentrate on books or anything else. The pieces of the puzzle felt like the pieces of my shattered brain, slowly being assembled and put together again. Luckily, I had my CD player and headphones with me and some 'chillout' CDs and I used this to help me cope and blot out the noises of the hospital.

I saw someone knitting, and asked for some knitting to do. I was only permitted to knit when I was being supervised, but later on I bought some children's soft plastic knitting needles so that I could pick up my knitting whenever I wanted to do it. This was extremely therapeutic; the repetitive action of knitting seems to be just right when my brain is numb and not thinking properly. I did not need to knit anything elaborate, just a simple garter stitch (a succession of 'knit' rows) and the action of the knitting needles were sufficient to keep me occupied.

The hospital had a quiet, carpeted sitting room with lovely big sofas where you could sit and just think. I was never forced into anything I did not want to do, and there were no large therapy groups. The nurses phoned my mother who advised them that I probably had AS and that I was sensitive to sudden noises, and, as a result, the ward alarm was switched to silent (a light flashed instead) so that I was not startled every time it was used.

There were three problematic aspects; the first was the dining hall. This had a lino floor and the wooden tables and chairs scraping on the floor and the terrible echoes in this room badly agitated my nerves. But the nurses were kind, and if the acoustics of this room got too much, I was allowed to take a tray to my room and eat my meal in a more peaceful setting. Later on, I became more tolerant of the noise and no longer needed to eat in my room.

The second difficulty was the queue for medication. For some reason, I am not good at queues, even when well. It seems difficult to maintain my balance and the press of people all around me is disturbing. Furthermore, if fellow patients were complaining about their treatment, I seemed to take it 'on board' and started to become upset. This time I developed a 'queue strategy'. I would find a comfortable seat in line of sight of the queue. I read a book or magazine so that it did not look as though I was deliberately avoiding the queue. Then, when there was only one patient left in the queue, I would join in at the end. Problem solved – 'queue nerves' dealt with.

The third hassle was the launderette for washing our own clothes. This caused immense stress out of all proportion to the task in hand.

I did not understand how the machines worked or how to program them to wash my clothes correctly using the symbols on the machine. I did not know where the washing powder came from, and I became worried that I did not know how long a cycle would take and did not want anyone else to empty the drum in my absence. On looking back, this was most odd, as I have successfully used public launderettes extensively in the past. Again, a kind patient came to my aid and set me straight, but a laminated instruction guide might have helped me solve these issues.

Smoking was not allowed in the ward and a room had been set aside for the smokers, so I did not have to cope with the smell of smoke. On a shopping trip I discovered some lavender aromatherapy bath soap and matching lavender pillow spray. About four days after my admission I noticed that I had problems sleeping, but I knew what to do to help me sleep. I took a warm bath or shower using the aromatherapy suds about half an hour before being ready to sleep, and sprayed my pillow with the lavender spray. Hot chocolate was offered as a night drink, and I made sure I had some before retiring. I selected a book from the hospital library and used my torch to read it to help me calm down and sleep without disturbing the other patients (I had been moved into an eight-bed ward after two days in the observation room).

The therapists loaned me their copy of Mark Haddon's book *The Curious Incident of the Dog in the Night-time* to read. It had only just been published and I was delighted to have the opportunity to read it; there was a small garden just outside the ward where I could sit and read undisturbed.

The whole culture in the hospital was supportive and calm; the patients were kind and helpful. Someone tried to taunt me about my liking for Buddhism, but I took it in good heart and later we became the best of friends.

In fact, laughter really helped me get through the experience. There is not much to smile about in a mental health in-patient facility, so someone who has a happy disposition makes a refreshing change. I would laugh as I struggled to get the washing machine to work, or if I did something bizarre I would say it was due to my 'silly brain' not working properly. I found that making light of my issues helped others around me to relax and maybe think that perhaps they were not faring as bad as I was. I soon found that the patients and staff warmed to me, and one quiet sunny Sunday when not much was going on I organised an impromptu picnic in the garden. Lots of people joined in, we had fresh cool squash to drink, someone brought a guitar and we arranged chairs and blankets to sit on and had a sing-song in the sun.

All in all for me the episode was a positive event. After I returned to Norfolk, my employers finally accepted that I was not going to be fit enough to work in London and I was medically retired, a result that was satisfactory for all involved.

Since then I have been on a course of group therapy to help me build up my confidence – it was run by women for women with all sorts of different problems. Again, I was nervous of attending a group scheme as I thought my communication difficulties would let me down; but I explained all this to my facilitators and they took this into account. This has been excellent therapy and helped to get me out of the house.

As well as this, I enrolled with an employment service which helps those on incapacity benefit prepare for working life. I tried a work placement as an activities organiser in a retirement home, but I discovered, much to my surprise, that this was most unsuitable. My face-recognition problems meant that I was unable to distinguish one resident from another, and my confidence was not robust enough to present a calm and reassuring face to my clients.

But later I tried a placement in a health food store and alternative therapy clinic. This was perfect. The shop smelled wonderful and put me at ease, and my computer skills were put to good use in the computerised diary booking system and accountancy work. My employers were so pleased with my work that I have now been taken on in a part-time paid position.

I have also studied for a Sage Accountancy qualification with Pitman's and gained a distinction; and now have a sheaf of other computing qualifications to add to my CV.

I have included three appendices that I hope will be useful for other people who have been in my position – or who might be.

APPENDIX 1. The lessons learnt: Some dos and don'ts

Have an 'emergency/comfort pack' with you if you think that the event/function you are scheduled to attend is going to be stressful. For example mine consists of the following:

- An MP3 player pre-loaded with favourite 'chillout' tracks – or anything that I think will calm me down. There is also a relaxation/meditation programme on mine. There is no excuse for not purchasing such a device these days, I have seen 1 gigabyte models for as little as £30, and, if you do not have a computer to download your tracks, you can use a computer in a library for this.

- A small bottle of Bach Flower rescue remedy spray.

- Some aromatherapy cream with your favourite calming scent – Boots now have a good range. Remember to use it. If a strong smell is upsetting you and you want to mask it, dab a little of the cream just under your nostrils. If you are anything like me then odours and smells are more important to your well-being than you might think. Be careful with neat essential oils as these are very strong and could cause a burn – dilute them down in a carrier oil such as almond oil.

- A list of contacts and addresses, especially the phone number of your GP.

- A collection of photographs of your favourite places and people.

- A copy of a Self-affirmation Pledge – modified for your own use (see Appendix 3).

- A small fluffy toy or memento given to you by someone who means a lot to you.

- A souvenir from a happy event or location you enjoy, perhaps an acorn from a favourite wood or a shell from a special beach.

- A piece of fabric (mine is velvet) that you find reassuring to touch. Have this in your pocket for tactile therapy.

- A 500ml bottle of drink; chilled, still water from the fridge is best. This helps me when I become so stressed that my mouth goes dry.

- A pair of soft foam ear plugs.

If for any reason you do find yourself in hospital, remember the following:

- Even today it is highly unlikely that you will find anyone who knows anything about AS.

- It does not matter that nursing staff are not familiar with AS. You are in hospital for a reason, and it is their job to make you better. Their strategies to deal with your distress, anxiety or disorientation will work whether you have AS or not.

- The hospital staff are not mind readers. If you have particular problems or triggers that make you uneasy and nervous, you must tell them about them. If at all possible, get a relative, friend, social worker, teacher to advocate for you.

- Co-operate, even if you think you would not like what has been offered as your therapy. You may be surprised at how well it goes.

- Try and find the quietest room on the ward and make use of it.

- Take out the items from your emergency pack; looking at the photographs and the small souvenirs will help you think your way back to happier times.

- If another patient is upset and staff are in attendance, try to distance yourself from the incident. Ideally find somewhere outdoors or out of earshot. This may seem to be cruel and unfeeling of you, but I know from experience that if I am having a crisis of some sort it is much better for me if there are fewer people around looking on. Furthermore, I believe that our senses are programmed such that alarm/distress in other people is contagious; if you put distance between yourself and the incident you will be protecting your own well-being.

- Remember that other patients may be more frightened of you than you are of them; try to talk to people to defuse this phenomenon. The safest topic is the weather. Remember to smile, even if you find this challenging. It will lighten your mood and people respond positively to a smile.

- Laughter really is the best medicine. It will be difficult at first, but if you can manage it at all, try and laugh at some of your symptoms. It will defuse the situation and help you and those around you to relax.

- If you have difficulty with eye contact, try to focus on an eyebrow or a forehead instead.

- Use your MP3 player discreetly and scent from your comfort pack to surround yourself in your own security 'bubble'.

- Try to avoid the medication queue as you will find this will add to your stress.

- Sleep is important. You must get enough sleep. If the ward is noisy at night, wear your soft foam earplugs from your emergency kit.

- Avoid any drinks containing caffeine before bedtime.

- If you are having difficulty sleeping, establish a regular night-time routine, take a scented bath or shower, have a hot chocolate drink, and spray your pillow with a calming scent.

- Make sure you have enough to drink. Buy a 500ml bottle of still spring water and refill your bottle from the ward's chilled water fountain if there is one in the vicinity. Carry your bottle with you at all times. Stress together with the medication causes a dry mouth, and having a dry mouth causes more stress. It's a vicious circle and you need to be equipped at all times to break that circle. Fizzy drinks are expensive and often have chemicals in them to make you want more; cool, still water is the best solution to this problem. Trust me on this one, I've been there and know it works!

APPENDIX 2. Helpful notes for therapists and nurses

You might get a better result if the therapy is delivered in a small group.

Remember a person with AS may have different tastes to those who are neurotypical. For example, trying dance therapy in a large group for me back in 1984 was, on reflection, not a very wise choice.

If at all possible wear a name badge with your name and job description – for example, 'Peter Smith – Staff nurse'. Remember to introduce yourself (and say what your job is) each time you meet with the patient and do not be offended if the patient with AS does not recognise you; they may be having difficulties distinguishing you from other staff, especially if their stress levels are high.

If there is a quiet room on the ward, make sure that the person with AS is aware of its location (you may need to actually show them the way a couple of times until the patient becomes familiar with the route). Encourage the patient to make use of the quiet room. This action alone may make life much easier for you, the AS patient and other patients on the ward.

Try not to use irony, sarcasm or figures of speech. This will only confuse the patient with AS and you will not make progress.

People with AS are, by their very nature, helpful individuals and eager to please. If the patient resists intervention, try to make it look as though they will be helping you if they take part. For example if a patient shows reluctance to take part in the suggested therapeutic activity, start the activity yourself and then ask the patient to help you finish it.

Therapies that are not too complicated and involve repetitive actions such as jigsaw puzzles, knitting, a yo-yo, or noughts and crosses will help to distract your patient and assist them to collect their thoughts together.

You may find that the patient likes to rock to and fro whilst sitting in a chair. This will probably look alarming, but the rocking action is calming to the patient and will reassure them.

If the ward has an alarm, try to work with the alarm on silent.

If the patient is very distressed, try to avoid using rooms that are acoustically noisy – as the echoes from the walls may disorientate and confuse them.

Remember that strategies you take to ameliorate symptoms in a person with AS may simultaneously help other patients, too.

APPENDIX 3. Self-affirmation Pledge

I am not defective. I am different.

I will not sacrifice my self-worth for peer acceptance.

I am a good and interesting person.

I will take pride in myself.

I am capable of getting along with society.

I will ask for help when I need it.

I am a person who is worthy of others' respect and acceptance.

I will find a career interest that is well suited to my abilities and interests.

I will be patient with those who need time to understand me.

I am never going to give up on myself.

I will accept myself for who I am.

I am confident.

Modified from *The Complete Guide to Asperger's Syndrome* by Tony Attwood (2007)

Chapter 2

Coping with Depression: Positive Advice for Aspies

Debbie Allan

Introduction by Luke Beardon
This chapter highlights just how much of an influence a working environment can have on the mental health of a person with AS. The world of employment is a scary one at best for many people with AS; an environment that does not protect the person with AS from bullying and discrimination is one which may lead to destruction of the individual and directly lead to mental ill health. It is of paramount importance that all employers of people with AS take mental health seriously; after all, employees with no mental health problems benefit everyone, not just the individual. By disregarding the impact of colleagues and other employment-related issues is to risk exposing employees with AS to mental torture and distress. Debbie's chapter illuminates this with great clarity.

My depression

I am 46 and I have suffered from moderate depression since I was about 20. I always found it strange how I was reasonably happy and contented when I was at school, but whenever I left I began to get quite depressed. As the years went on, I found that despite putting a great deal of effort into improving my social abilities I didn't seem to notice much improvement. When I put an effort into other things like studying a subject, or learning a practical skill I would see a good improvement in my ability. It frustrated me that even when I put myself in uncomfortable situations over and over to try and get better at dealing with people I still felt really uncomfortable talking to them and was aware they felt uneasy talking to me.

I became aware there were some work- and non-work-related tasks I just couldn't do accurately but which other people seemed to be able to do easily, such as sorting out orders and deliveries, and I made many mistakes completing forms and recording information. I found that no matter how much effort I put into getting these things right I seemed always to make mistakes. I began to get into trouble for these things and was told to take more care. I was often told that although everyone makes mistakes I make a lot more than most people. I was often completely flummoxed at how I could have made some of the mistakes as the things I was doing weren't that difficult. I seemed to have a serious lack of concentration.

As many years went past, I became less and less confident in my ability to do many tasks and became more and more convinced that I couldn't do anything right. I also felt down because of the 'block' I seemed to have conversing with people, and confusion about why this was still happening. I remember a colleague saying to me that he thought I was very intelligent but had no common sense. The odd thing was I thought the complete opposite i.e. that although I wasn't very bright at least I had good common sense.

I believed I was of very low intelligence and had thought so ever since I was young. I had a feeling in my head of being slow or slightly mentally retarded. The thing that confused me was that occasionally I felt like my mind was sharp the way a normal person's must be, but a large amount of the time I felt I was thinking through a fog.

After a long number of years in my first job, I was relocated due to cutbacks, and this move turned out to be a horrendous experience and I was bullied terribly by all five people I worked with. I didn't realise at the time how depressed I was and I just seemed to keep plugging on. I used most of my annual leave and public holidays to go on a day-release class which I enjoyed, but my workmates seemed threatened by my doing this, which didn't help with the bullying situation. It did help in other ways i.e. by giving me one day away from the place, and the group in my college class were nice and friendly. They would even invite me to the pub afterwards until their train was due and seemed to like my company.

I was continually transferred from one department to the next every year or so and told I wasn't fitting in. In each place I went to I was bullied, and although I was a high grade I was given the most menial tasks to do and new untrained staff just out of school were given more responsible tasks to do than me. It was obviously being done to try and demoralise me. Then one day out of the blue after being in this job for 18 years I was told that 'my ability to do my job had been brought into question'. I discovered a case to have me dismissed was being put together between the Seniors in all the areas I'd been sent to. Most of what was written down about me was lies including wrong dates, but at the time my self-esteem was so low I just believed them. I was dismissed with no redundancy money.

Leading up to this I became very depressed, was put on one anti-depressant after another as well as anti-psychotic medicines and was eventually admitted to a psychiatric ward and stayed for one month.

It was not until many years later that I was contacted by other people who worked in the same job and I discovered that I was the first of many who lost their job by a similar method. The only difference was that none of them put up with the bullying for longer than a few months and just accepted it and left. The turmoil they went through didn't go on for long, unlike me where it seemed to go on for years. A big difference between the others who lost their jobs and myself is that they didn't for a minute believe the management's claims that they were incompetent were even slightly true, but I believed every word of it.

So not only had I lost my long-term job and had a mortgage to keep paying, but my self-esteem was at rock bottom. In hindsight I now know that, in comparison to many of my colleagues, I was good at most aspects of the job and also very meticulous with my work, and that some staff from other departments would only let me work on their projects for that reason. There were a few tasks I wasn't good at, but not everything.

For a number of years afterwards I was very frightened to go near the area where I'd worked even although it wasn't far from my home. I was also left very paranoid and still am to this day. I am sure that every nice-seeming person I come across will turn against me as that seems to have been the way of my adult working life. One man told me when I went to tell him I'd been sacked that he was really sorry to have put a bad word in about me but he would have lost his job if he didn't. Ironically he was the next one to be paid off. All along this man was telling me what he was being asked to do by the management, which included him being called to a meeting and notes dictated to him of what he was to write about me for the Personnel Officer.

I am no longer working now as after that job I worked in a long succession of jobs and encountered many difficulties in doing certain tasks and in my relationships with colleagues. I am always very nervous and jumpy and waiting for my colleagues to criticise me, and whenever a workmate is near to me when I'm working I can't concentrate for feeling so nervous. In some jobs I've got on well with the staff especially when it was a smaller group, but in others I had a terrible time. Also certain tasks which I was good at in one job, I'd be useless at in another, which I couldn't understand.

My last job was in a hospital laboratory, which was a very high-pressure environment and staff were very ambitious and competitive. As I was a trainee in this job just about every other person was bossing me about, which I could have put up with but one woman who was known to be a terrible bully picked up on my lack of speed under pressure and made my time there horrendous. I already felt quite low as to why, again, I seemed to make more mistakes than the other people despite concentrating very hard; they seemed to talk and laugh whilst doing their work and yet managed to get it right. I knew in the back of my mind that I would never be competent enough to be left on my own, for example on night duty, and felt disaster was looming. My training kept getting delayed and yet the other three trainees were being trained away ahead of me. Whenever I asked the reason for this, excuses were made and nothing was ever said to me about my ability to do the job. I became more and more nervous and ill and I eventually had to go on permanent sick leave. I knew from my previous job when I had ended up really ill and in hospital that I was quickly approaching that stage again, i.e. beginning to feel quite suicidal, so had to get out.

I have now not worked for about three years and for most of this time I have not been depressed at all. I have been a bit anxious about my finances but not depressed and frightened by a person's actions. About a year ago I was diagnosed with Asperger syndrome, which at first was a shock but a relief in the end and an explanation of why some tasks I could do well in one job seemed to prove impossible for me in another. I've also met lots of nice friendly people who have Asperger's and don't have to rely on people who were using me to be friends. I still have a few of my original pals though. I also no longer feel guilty in myself about not being able to do some things but get a bit down when family members think my diagnosis is rubbish.

I have come to the conclusion only recently that much of my depression has been caused by my lack of assertiveness and the reason for my lack of assertiveness has been believing I was odd in comparison to others and a second-class citizen. It is only in the last year or so that I have really made a big effort to become assertive and not put up with being used and pushed around by people, and I think my self-esteem has improved. If you are a quiet person, it is even more important to practise assertiveness as bullies assume you are easy pickings.

I think when you spend your week in a job where there is a great amount of stress then it is important to do something you enjoy at the weekends and not to go out clubbing or to pubs if it is not your thing just to keep your friends happy. I put myself in situations I hated often to keep friendly with my pal from my school days. I know this didn't help my self-esteem over the years. I also went on holiday to Spain with the friend and felt I was in a trance for the days I was there. I was crying most of the time, and eventually someone in the holiday company arranged a flight home. My friend thought it normal for young people to sleep all day and spend all night in discos in the hope of finding a man. I just went along with what was expected as whenever I tried to persuade her to do things differently she made me out to be abnormal.

I think in order to maintain good mental health it is important to be good to yourself and not to let others tell you what to do all the time. If someone wants to do a particular activity and you agree to it, then they should be prepared to do something you enjoy the next time. The problem I have found has been that I haven't had many friends so rather than risk losing one I've just gone along with what they wanted, which was me being very disrespectful to myself. I was embarrassed to admit that I enjoyed looking after my animals and doing my various crafts as it didn't seem to be the right thing for a young person to be doing. I was told this often by my boss and other people. It is only now at the age of 46 that I've got to the stage I have 'had enough' of always being the one to compromise and be controlled by people, and I have become much more assertive.

I still seem to fight a constant battle against people trying to take advantage of me, as I seem to have this hidden rule in my head that you must put others' wishes before your own and feel that I am a bad person if I don't. I think this again stems from having very few friends and reading countless books on how to be a good friend and the fear of losing any I make. Putting others before yourself all the time must be very bad for your confidence – it's as though it doesn't matter if you are unhappy as long as the other person is.

Another thing probably relating to Asperger syndrome which hasn't helped me is not taking the initiative and that is something I try to do now. When I am out with any friends instead of saying 'I don't mind' when something is suggested I try to say what I would like to do next. I have noticed other people with Asperger's do the same thing, i.e. just wait for everyone else to make a decision and then everyone is saying 'I don't mind'!

The thing is I always believed that my work was a major cause of the depression I suffered from, but if you want to have a decent standard of living then you have to work. So it's a difficult situation and I had no idea that some of the jobs I worked in would not be easy for someone with AS.

Things that help

There are a number of things that have helped me handle the depression and paranoia, including going for nice walks in the evening on my own looking at the gardens and flowers, cats, etc. and just letting my mind go without having to concentrate on talking to someone.

I took a lot of part-time college courses during my working life and whenever any of these came to an end I always noticed my mood would go down fairly quickly. I couldn't ever seem to control this and would always end up enrolling for another course and the depression would once again reduce itself. These courses also gave me something else in my mind and something to talk about to colleagues, although some colleagues didn't seem happy at the idea that I might become more highly qualified than them. Some of the courses were work-related and others were leisure courses.

I have recently made a great big effort to be more assertive and less frightened of what people (who don't mean anything to me) think of me. I am determined not to be taken advantage of now and have noticed some of the most difficult people in my life are no longer having such a controlling effect on me. Now I have quite a few nice people I know with AS I feel more able to stand up to the non-AS people I know without fear of losing their friendship. I think if people have been used to controlling you for a long time then it takes quite a lot of persistence to make it clear they are not going to get away with it any more. I have read many books over the years on how to gain confidence, but you get so much advice it's hard to know what will work. So after I left my last job I decided to make a big effort with assertiveness, as I had a feeling that could be one of the reasons for my lack of confidence.

I also now try to laugh at any funny things that happen (not at other people) but just in general to me, or I kid my friends as I've heard that is a form of affection. I like to see someone with a very serious face turn into a big smile and know I caused that to happen. If I hear someone coming out with a funny line, I often try and remember it. Often if I say something funny, the other person says something funny back, and I end up laughing and it leaves me with a good feeling.

I have always found my pets help me a lot, although I have quite low-maintenance pets; I have a pair of budgies so they can entertain each other and I don't feel guilty going out and leaving them. There is something about caring for them and watching them that takes my mind off things temporarily, and in my work I often used to think about them.

I find just meeting friends for a coffee or for short periods of time on a regular basis helps me and puts other thoughts in my head. I have met a few people through the various mental health projects I've gone to.

Another thing that has helped me a little which I've often read about is to speak to myself in a caring way when things are bad and imagine I'm someone else talking, i.e. a nice kind sort of person and not a critical one. My psychiatrist told me once that people with depression need to be much nicer to themselves and give themselves lots of nice treats. I love a soak in a bath with bubbly baths and things.

When I was young I had a great hobby which took me all over the UK now and again, and I think a hobby where you can meet others with similar interests is great. I bred gerbils and at that time many new coat colours were appearing, and I loved this hobby. It's good to have a hobby which you can enjoy on your own but which also allows you to meet others who have the same interest.

I try to eat lots of fruit and vegetables although I also eat many other things I enjoy too. I find doing exercise difficult as having depression and Asperger's I think makes it difficult to get the motivation. I went swimming once a week for about five years and now no longer swim but play badminton with other AS people.

I need a lot of sleep and something I find very difficult is resisting having a nap during the day. Although I am not depressed now I still get a quite tired and 'frazzled' feeling especially when I've been amongst company all day. I think it takes quite a long time to calm your brain down for someone with AS and I find it is just racing even although nothing very stressful has happened. To get rid of this feeling I have to go for a quiet walk away from crowds of people and noise or else meet a pal for a quiet chat. I think this is one of the most difficult things I have to deal with just now, i.e. trying to keep my head feeling calm and not letting people's nastiness go round and round in my thoughts. I think meditation or yoga is a good thing if you can practise it.

I now have an opportunity to meet up with other people on the spectrum and go on outings and do enjoyable things, and that has really helped my mental health.

Keeping busy and having a routine is definitely a great thing for me and I have a mental health project to go to at least three days of the week. The other two days I have things to do as well, but for a long time I was getting depressed at the weekends. About two months ago I decided to make a big effort to plan something to do for each weekend, and so far I have kept it up. This means I don't lie in so long and it has had the effect of taking away the depression over the weekend. Sometimes it isn't easy to think of what to do, but every so often there is some event on that I now look forward to or something to get me out of my bed, and it definitely helps.

I think being on your own too much must be a bad thing for any mental health problem; it's okay to do that if you have AS and are not depressed, but meeting people even just for a short time each day makes a great difference to my mood. Even just passing someone in the street that I know and talking to them for five minutes can change my day from being a down day to an okay day.

Chapter 3

My Fur-lined Bucket: Alternative Methods for Dealing with Mental Health Issues

E. Veronica Bliss

Introduction by Luke Beardon
Vicky's perspective on life is a refreshing one that has its dark undertones. Despite her superb writing style including a wonderful sense of humour, it is clear that, alongside others in this book, she has suffered at the hands of other professionals who have not understood her.

In a similar vein to Janet's story (Chapter 1) Vicky notes that not adapting perspectives to take AS into account is potentially detrimental to the individual. AS must be taken into account by all professionals involved, or else there is a high chance of misunderstandings and miscommunications.

In addition to highlighting the need for AS to be taken into account, Vicky writes about people trying to change her. So many people with AS, on entering mental health services, are faced with a similar issue: change must come from within. However, if the root of the problem is not from within – but from the external environment – then expecting the individual to change is both inappropriate and potentially damaging. This is quite aside from the fact that many of the changes expected are ones which are impossible for the individual with AS in any circumstances!

Vicky advocates for 'solution focused brief therapy' for people with AS. Her book authored with Genevieve Edmonds (2007) is an excellent read for anyone interested in finding out more about this process of support.

I wonder what it is? This thing or condition called mental health? And does it have any descriptive properties where I am concerned?

Described one way, I am falling-down tired and laughing inappropriately at the destruction of my own private property; I am self-harming; whenever I am awake, I have mental noise of confusing and unhappy thoughts racing in loops and twists; I do not follow conventional wisdom about the use of prescription medications; I find the process of just doing everyday things exhausting; several times a week I feel deeply depressed by and angry at the things I see people do to one another; sometimes I sit quietly with a specially made bucket on my head; my very favourite place to be is underneath a pile of small animals (live ones I mean, I am not *that* morbid) or wrapped around horses. So. *Am* I mentally healthy?

To look at the same thing another way however, I somehow keep putting one foot in front of the other even though I am falling-down tired; I am laughing at the destruction of my own property because I care more about my living, breathing, clumsy, silly puppy than I do about the property he is destroying; I am self-harming by eating my own body weight in ice cream because I am presently obsessed with the stuff; even though I have chronic mental noise, I get up and try to do something useful for myself or someone else every damned day; I am confident enough to make my own decisions regarding the use of prescription medications; even though the behaviour of the general public saddens me because it is, to me, so unnecessarily hurtful, I have not become homicidal; my head-bucket was specially made for me by my very good friend – it is comfortably lined with fur and has a face on the outside (so I can appear socially appropriate *and* have an autistic trip) and I only use the bucket in private – never ever whilst driving; I am able to both draw comfort from and give comfort to animals almost unconditionally. So. *Am* I mentally healthy?

Describe me to a mental health professional using the first paragraph and my guess is that I will be tentatively diagnosed as mentally unwell, and at high risk of further mental deterioration. Use the second paragraph though, and it is more likely I will be thought of as eccentric but passable as mentally healthy. In other words, describe to most mental health professionals a half-empty glass and they will tell you that you are thirsty. Describe a glass half full and they will more likely send you on your way. Given that both describe the same state of being, mental health seems to me to be quite a rickety concept.

I like mental health professionals as a breed. I am one after all, and I have experienced how the system works from both sides of the desk. Mental health is defined by the person in any given room who has most of the power. I guess, for example, that there is an unwritten rule for the majority of people about sitting quietly with one's head in a bucket. I further guess that this rule says that people who wear buckets are abnormal and that such people ought to have more acceptable ways of coping with whatever traumas and dramas come along. Typically it is seen as the mental health professional's job to point this out, and to help the person remove the bucket and face the world in a socially acceptable way. More often than not, the client comes to see a mental health professional for precisely this kind of advice or direction, having been convinced by other people in power that bucket-wearing is not normal. Or perhaps the use of the bucket is making the client feel worse rather than better, so they seek an alternative way to behave from the mental health team. If both the mental health professional and the client agree that the bucket has to go, then a happy and probably productive therapeutic relationship will follow.

What I have sometimes seen happen though is that the mental health professional decides bucket-wearing is not good and sets about trying to change it even though the bucket is useful and pleasant for the client. Bucket-wearing is easily seen as not normal, and mental health professionals are pretty much trained to help people become normal. They may feel they did not do their job if their client still has a bucket on their head even after several sessions of therapy. The client, on the other hand, may have improved in self-confidence through therapy and be thus *even more* inclined to wear the bucket when they feel the need. The therapist feels unsatisfied, the client feels good – but is the client mentally healthy?

People with AS seem particularly susceptible to this kind of 'professional knows best' approach from mental health workers.

Many things that are normal for a person with AS are not considered normal by the majority of the population. Thus family, friends, professionals, employers, teachers and so on frequently feel there is something 'wrong' with the AS person. Because there is no obvious physical problem, it is guessed that the problem – the abnormality – is mental in nature. This happens to other minority groups too. It is certainly not just people with AS who are thought to be abnormal when measured by the standard 'norms'. So when a person with AS comes through the therapy door, the mental health worker will have no trouble immediately identifying a list of thoughts, behaviours or feelings that appear outside the range of 'normal'. So many aspects of the AS person may appear broken that the question in the therapist's mind is likely not to be one of 'What should I do?' so much as it is 'Blimey! Where do I start?'

Because of the unique way information is processed by people with AS, confusion or misunderstandings often occur between the mental health worker and the AS client. If the worker is not familiar with the AS person's need for clear expectations, literal language use, sameness, etc. these are more likely to be seen as symptoms of illness rather than differences in mental processes. People with AS get labels of 'difficult', 'resistant to change', 'unable to form a relationship', 'unable to benefit from therapy' and so on because the way they use language is different from the 'norm'. When a typical mental health professional gets a whiff of abnormality, they are trained to dig for the reason behind this problem. They look for pathology (an underlying cause, deficiency or disease) that will explain the AS client's abnormal behaviour, when actually the behaviour seen as abnormal by the worker is perfectly functional and normal for the client. This being the case, it seems lots of mentally healthy people with AS get unnecessarily labelled as mentally unhealthy due to a lack of understanding from the mental health worker.

When I was training as a psychologist in America, I was privileged to work alongside some lovely, top notch people. I appreciated their skills and knowledge and worked hard to learn every scrap of information that was on offer. They also worked hard to change me, because in every evaluation my inability to 'feel' or to identify emotions was highlighted as suspect. Professors of psychology are reliable in their habit of questioning students 'And how did you feel when the client said this?' or 'How did you feel when your mother said that?' and blow me I could never get the answer to those questions right. Nor could I work out a way to cheat and copy the answers from someone else. Apparently, because of some deep-seated problems in my early life, I intellectualised everything. That means that my professors and colleagues convinced me that I had shut off my emotions, probably because of some gooey trauma that I was now repressing, and that I developed an intellectual approach to interacting with other people. Jeepers. Answers on a postcard if anyone can tell me what 'intellectualising' means. I felt seriously flawed and I scrambled around furiously trying to de-intellectualise myself and start feeling. Naturally I went to therapy because I was broken, abnormal and I was frightened witless that I had a past trauma to uncover. The mental health professionals who were pointing out my deficits were not horrible people – they were rather nice, respectable people, doing what they had been trained to do; find a problem and dig it out. Only thing is, they got to define 'problem' and I, in the weaker position of learner, got to accept their assessment and work on my 'problem'.

That was in the late 1980s. Twenty years on, I realise I never had a problem! What I have is a difference in the way I mentally manipulate information. I've been through my personal history forwards, backwards, sideways and other ways, and there is no deep-seated repression of some dark gooey trauma. The best I can come up with is that when making my school lunches mum used to cut my sandwiches lengthways and dad cut them sideways – that little change in routine was pretty tough to take it's true, but it did not, I am happy to say, scar me for life. If my professors and colleagues could have been satisfied just noticing that I was different from them, without having to make that difference a bad or sick thing, I'd have rolled merrily along, probably without a history of therapy, medications and diagnoses. I probably would still like wearing my fur-lined bucket though, because my bucket is not a product of mental illness, it's just fun.

Excuse me now whilst I just get my soap box out…

There now. I am settled on my solution focused brief therapy (de Shazer *et al.* 1986) pedestal, overlooking all other types of therapy (everyone who knows me has just heaved a great sigh and put their heads in their hands because they know what is coming). *Solution focused brief therapy is the bee's knees for people with AS!* It is a respectful way of approaching the differences between therapist and client, and an SF worker does not seek to identify or fix a 'problem'. An SF worker instead listens for what is already working for the client (in my earlier scenario, my bucket-wearing) and together with the client they try to work out how the client can do more of what is working. Thus, in a solution focused session, spending time with a bucket on one's head is seen as an adaptive thing – a creative, clever solution to the trauma of daily life – rather than something 'not normal'. If I, as the AS client, wanted to rid myself of the bucket, the therapist would help me do that, but if I like the bucket (as I clearly do) the SF worker would not suggest that this was a character flaw which needed fixing. All the useful little quirks, taps, flaps, spins, hops and flicks that we do so very well can be considered quite normal within the context of solution focused brief therapy. Imagine that! A place where the AS client isn't considered abnormal just because they are AS! What a great idea!

I won't go on about solution focused approaches because there are other publications that do that quite well (e.g. Bliss 2005; Bliss and Edmonds 2007; O'Connell 2005; O'Connell and Palmer 2003). I think in terms of mental health and AS, I certainly have differences which have led to diagnoses of mental ill health and at the same time, I am quite mentally healthy thank you very much. Me, here under my fur-lined bucket... with a cat and two dogs on my lap... and horses just outside the window... I am just fine.

References

Bliss, E.V. (2005) 'Common factors, a solution focus and Sarah.' *Journal of Systemic Therapies* 24, 4, 16–31.

Bliss, E.V. and Edmonds, G. (2007) *A Self-Determined Future and Asperger Syndrome: A Solution Focused Approach.* London: Jessica Kingsley Publishers.

de Shazer, S., Berg, I.K., Lipchick, E., Nunnally, E., Molnar, A., Gingrich, W. and Weiner-Davis, M. (1986) 'Brief therapy: Focused solution development.' *Family Process 25*, 207–222.

O'Connell, B. (2005) *Solution-Focused Therapy* (2nd edn). London: Sage.

O'Connell, B. and Palmer, S. (eds) (2003) *Handbook of Solution-focused Brief Therapy.* London: Sage.

Chapter 4

This Aspie Life: The Undiagnosed Aspie Experience

8Ball

Introduction by Luke Beardon
8ball's writing is superb. The mix of dry humour and honest language is a delight to read – or would be if it were not for the very serious nature of mental ill health that is the topic for discussion. I will let 8ball's eloquence speak for itself. Suffice to say that 8ball is an exemplary example of how to explode the myths that people with AS cannot communicate effectively and do not have a sense of humour.

This does raise a very important point regarding AS and mental health, and that is of the very skilful ability of many people with AS to mask the very real mental health issues that they encounter. So many people with AS appear to be 'coping' when in actual fact there is a need for support and recognition of fundamental issues affecting their lives. Many people with AS are expert actors/actresses – so called echopraxic behaviour can be an excellent coping mechanism for how to behave in unknown situations, but it can also mask what is going on internally. Professionals must develop the ability to spot what is going on beneath the surface for some individuals to recognise that support needs are required, rather than assuming all is fine based on an external presentation of an individual.

Introduction

Having checked back to see what it is I'm supposed to be writing here, it seems this is a piece about mental *health* rather than one about mental *illness*.

That's a shame really, because I have more experience of the latter than the former when I really think about it, but needs must, so I'll begin with a definition (all definitions nicked directly or paraphrased from Wikipedia, by the way):

> *Mental health* is a term used to describe either a level of cognitive or emotional wellbeing or an absence of mental illness.

Well, that makes it easier, the definition seems to mean your brain is functioning more-or-less properly, you're in no obvious emotional distress, and you're free from...

> *Mental illness*: A mental illness or mental disorder refers to one of many mental health conditions characterised by distress, impaired cognitive functioning, atypical behaviour, emotional dysregulation, and/or maladaptive behaviour.

This is more like my territory! Okay, so in layman's terms, mental illness means emotional distress, confused thinking, and acting strangely. Three simple ingredients that combined make the cake of madness.

Of course, everyone in life goes through emotional distress at some time or other, and sooner or later everyone does something that someone will interpret as odd and that will make people think they are not thinking entirely straight (NTs do this too but seem to have an in-built 'return to conformance' routine that means they can flip back to seeming 'normality' before triggering their fellow NTs' 'attack non-conformance' reflex [I can see I'm going to be needing more definitions soon]).[1]

As far as I can tell, mental illness is when you exhibit a pattern of these three traits that fits the profile in a book that is in the hands of what we jokingly refer to as 'medical professionals'.

---

1   Those without ASDs (autistic spectrum 'disorders') may feel a little lost at this point. Well you'll just have to deal with being puzzled for a bit – it's not like you ever went out of your way to explain your idiosyncratic rules and lexicon to me – you'll pick it up as you go along.

As far as I can tell, that is it – no urine or blood tests, no brain scans, no flashing strobelights in darkened rooms (you're lucky to even get an ink-blot test these days) – the only thing that can tell you if you're as stark raving mad as a box of frogs is a qualified medical practitioner.

Scary, huh? I wouldn't want to get on the wrong side of one of these guys…

Mental illness vs. AS

From the way certain social 'support' groups carry on you could be forgiven for thinking that AS *is* a mental illness (indeed, AS is in the DSM-IV[2] list of mental illnesses, but then so is epilepsy) so the opinion of these quacks can and should be discounted. Neil, in his bit (see Chapter 8), gave a great little rundown on why the mental illness paradigm is badly suited for use when thinking about AS.

My take is quite similar – I see AS as a neurological condition resulting from a variant arrangement of 'wiring' in the brain. So, rather than being compared to schizophrenia or panic disorder, say, it is more suited to being compared to being gay, or left-handed, or perhaps dyslexic.

Interestingly, these 'mis-wirings' appear to associate with each other quite commonly, as do some other traits which even the dreaded NTs see as desirable. It's been observed that left-handed people are more likely to be highly creative, highly intelligent, and have a higher incidence of homosexuality.[3] In my experience the same is true of Aspies.

Also, autistics are more often left-handed than the rest of the population. Reading up on this stuff has convinced me that what we are looking at here is not 'disorder', or 'illness', but simply a different way of being human.

My opinion, in summary: AS is far from unique in terms of being a variant form of brain-wiring. These differences in themselves are *not*

---

2   The DSM-IV (*Diagnostic and Statistical Manual*) is the US standard reference for psychiatry.

3   Though it was only 1974 that being gay was removed from the DSM-IV, and not so very long before that that left-handedness was seen a deviation that needed 'curing' – and these mis-classifications caused terrible and needless suffering to those affected by them.

what constitute mental illness *per se*, though those exhibiting these differences may show a higher reported incidence of mental illnesses, for reasons which I'll go into soon.

Experiments have shown that NTs can be made to 'go mad' if certain changes are made to their living conditions (solitary confinement being the big 'NT mind-killer') and the same is true of those with AS. However, we live in a world where the social environment is determined by and for NTs – and so Aspies, being in a minority, are a little lost when it comes to the invisible rituals and unspoken curriculum of this strange world, and often without access to encouragement and guidance from those with a shared perspective, can run into problems all the more easily.

I have no doubt that if societal conditions had been 'designed' by and for people with AS, someone would be writing a little essay on 'NT disorder' and how to cope with it. But they haven't, so they aren't, and I'm doing this one instead.

Hello, I'm 8ball

That's not my real name, by the way, that would be a cruel prank to play on a child, 8ball is just an internet alias I sometimes use. I'm a bit of a hermit and like to retain my semi-anonymity for a number of reasons. As far as this little essay goes, it serves an extra purpose since I have friends, work colleagues and family members that are not aware of my AS status.

Well, I say 'AS status', but I have no formal diagnosis. I was 'spotted' (if you will) by a friend-of-a-friend who has a brother with high-functioning autism, and noticed a whole bunch of similar traits in me. That was a couple of years ago now. It took some time for me to really come to terms with the fact that I am Aspie – I just kept thinking 'I can't be autistic – how ridiculous!' Sure, I'd always known something was different but then doesn't everyone think they're 'different' or 'special' in some way?

Also, I didn't want to feel 'defined' by the wiring in my head – since adolescence I'd worked very hard at constructing what others would find an acceptable 'persona', with varying degrees of success. I guess I thought I could wish a 'normal' person into existence, whose mantle I could take on without fear of ever being found out. For many of my teenage years the idea that one day things would be better was the one thing that sustained me through some very difficult times.

It was a great relief to find out that there were others like me, but it was also hard to let go of the idea that I'd never 'fix myself' – at least not in the way that I had always longed for.

Much as I thought I was a unique kind of freak until quite recently, the main points of my life with regard to AS and how it has affected my mental wellbeing are very typical of the undiagnosed Aspie experience:

- *childhood*: difficult, bullied, problems with authority
- *adolescence*: difficult, ostracised, unable to deal with teenage rituals and culture
- *young adulthood*: confusion, depression, problems finding a place in the world.

One thing that stands out from my little 'life summary', I suppose, is that nothing obviously 'mental health' related pops up until the last line. I suppose everything up until that point in life is preparation, really, so I felt quite comfortable with feeling 'incomplete' up until then, though when young adulthood came along, not only was a lot of the teenage checklist often still outstanding (due to the usual social interaction issues), but also the first task of adulthood – finding a place in the world and a purpose in life – loomed large, and I was acutely aware that I was getting left behind.

Finding a place and a purpose

It seems to me that adolescence and early adulthood is something of a 'mental health blackspot' for NTs and Aspies alike.

I'm sure there are many complex and intertwined factors that influence this, that far more learned types than myself have written books on the subject and that these factors include hormonal upheaval, neurological changes, binge drinking, happy-slapping, incipient syphilis, etc., etc. I think a lot of it is tied up with a person's childhood expectations of what adult life has in store for them.

Everyone starts off with certain expectations, involving finding a place and purpose in the world, where they expect to be, what social groups they will be a part of, etc. Sometimes a person will have quite well-defined expectations, such as those annoyingly focused kids who decide, seemingly at birth, that they want to be a doctor or whatever and later go to medical school and achieve their ambition. At the other extreme, sometimes a person won't have the faintest idea what they want to do with their life right into adulthood – as was the case with me. I guess most people probably aren't at either end of this spectrum and are pretty comfortable making things up as they go along.

As a child I'd become firmly preoccupied with several different ideas at various times, but for one reason or another[4] I found myself somewhat directionless in my teens. This may sound like a normal teenage thing for you, but I wasn't exactly a normal teenager – I was gullible, uncouth, awkward, shy, tactless… well, apart from those things I wasn't exactly a normal teen. The time came to make decisions about careers/university courses, and in a moment of haste/panic I took what turned out to be some rather dodgy career advice, scraped through a few exams and headed off to university, with an unrealistically rosy picture in my head of what student life would hold for me.

At university I was horribly overwhelmed – I knew I was socially awkward and had a few strategies up my sleeve for how to appear moderately 'normal', but these ploys really weren't up to the job of getting me through the more socially sophisticated world of university – all the rules had changed again. To compound this, the course I had enrolled on held no interest for me, I knew I'd made a mistake. And I was also plagued by problems with my health from the age of about 18 onwards. Some of these illnesses had doctors quite bemused, and I was accused of making things up on a number of occasions. It felt like my life was falling to pieces on both the inside and outside, and I had no idea how to fix things.

---

4   The main reason being the fall of the Berlin Wall on 9 November 1989 – for reasons too convoluted, and frankly *weird* to go into here.

I changed course after a year but the health and social issues persisted. I was lucky to make some great friends at university (when I think back, these were among the very first 'real' friends I ever had), who helped me through some very difficult times and made me feel like a real person when I could feel myself slipping away into the depths of depression.

That was a long time ago now – I got through it a day at a time, sometimes making reasonable decisions and sometimes screwing things up royally.

I guess I still don't really know what I want to do with my life – after university I felt I had had my fill of academia for the time being and drifted aimlessly for a few years. Nowadays I'm drifting ever-so-slightly more purposefully. At this rate I'll have made real inroads into the laundry before I'm found dead, alone and unloved, partially eaten by the next-door neighbour's chihuahua.[5]

Some things I've learned

For most of the time that I've been dealing with depression I was unaware of Asperger syndrome, so I don't know how many of the strategies I have come up with for controlling my depression and for getting through life in general are going to be quite idiosyncratic and specific to me only; some of them may be more applicable to dealing with depression in general than anything to do with AS.

That said, there may be something someone will find useful in here.

HUMOUR
Yes, groan, groan, I know...

I promise to get the clichés over right at the start (before perhaps returning to a couple at the end if I'm feeling a bit Jerry Springer). The usefulness of humour shouldn't be underestimated, though. I find if I can visualise myself raging internally at some traffic lights refusing to change I can quite quickly see how ridiculous I am being.

Also, humour is a great way of dealing with frustration, and frustration is a recurring theme in the Aspie experience. I think we

---

5   I still get a little morbid at times, in spite of the medication.

all forget what it's like to be a small child when everything is new and being learnt, and we were getting things wrong far more often than we got them right. When we were learning to speak our parents would hear our babbling and conclude we were 'learning to speak' rather than 'failing to speak', and when intelligible words came out we were rewarded rather than chided for not being born knowing everything. When we messed things up it wasn't held against us, and sometimes when the adults laughed at us we could see the funny side too.

Being older, it's easy to blame yourself for every mistake that happens, I guess we feel we should be 'complete' as adults and not still making faltering, child-like progress in the world. I still fall into this trap, but I also try to remember that I'm still learning, due in part to not having been born with the full hardwired NT skill set. And I find it helpful to take a step back, laugh at myself, and try to remember to do better next time rather than making myself feel inferior and useless.

KEEP REACHING OUT TO OTHERS
We all need time alone sometimes, people with AS more so than most, experiencing repeated rejections and bad experiences. I find it easy to become misanthropic and hide myself away after a few negative responses from people, but this isn't the best idea – people with AS are dependent on others just the same as everyone else – we just need to take more regular breaks.

People with AS, often having intense interests, can find friends with whom they share something in common by joining clubs and societies, but just sticking to these groups doesn't necessarily help with dealing with people in general. It's easily done, but I think it is essential to get out of your comfort zone every so often so that life does not begin to feel stagnant – you can always return to your comfort zone later if you want.

It can be scary, so I'd recommend taking a trusted NT friend when venturing into unknown territories, but it can enlarge your world and you may surprise yourself with what you are capable of. Many of my happiest memories and most valuable experiences have come from taking a chance and breaking away from the comfort of routine.

It's not always this rosy, though, negative experiences will happen. Sometimes it will be clumsiness or misjudgement on your part, or it may just be that someone you are trying to connect with has something else on their mind, other plans, or any number of things that are nothing directly to do with you. Much as they like to put on a show of strength, life is often difficult for NTs too – try not to judge them too harshly.

Sigmund Freud once said: 'One day in retrospect the years of struggle will strike you as the most beautiful.'

Keep reaching out to others.

WATCHING THE NTS AND STUDYING THEIR BEHAVIOUR

I mentioned before that as an adolescent I was often trying to create an acceptable 'persona' for myself. It never really occurred to be that 'being myself' (with some care taken to smooth out some of the rougher edges that NTs find off-putting) was an option. It would have been wonderful in those days to have known that there was nothing desperately wrong with me and that there were others going through similar experiences.

NTs have a strange group superstition – a bit like their much-loved 'common sense' myth – that their hardwired 'social skills'[6] are something that is an immutable part of a human being's essence which cannot be learnt, dissected, or convincingly replicated. Words like 'charisma' (which comes from the Greek for 'divine gift'), and terms like 'gift of the gab' and 'silver tongue' betray the line of thinking that an affinity for the social 'dance' is an in-born talent rather than a skill that can be learnt like reading, riding a bicycle, or programming a computer.

This idea is complete bunk, even the most basic mimicking of NT mannerisms such as their use of eye contact (looking between the eyes or at the nose can work if eye contact is particularly difficult for you), mirroring of body language, and keeping an eye out for

---

6   I have put the term 'social skills' in quote marks because as well as those better NT qualities that people with AS often lack (such as tact, understanding of personal space, the spooky knack of jumping into each other's minds without burning out), I am including the less admirable NT traits of manipulation, deceit, one-upmanship and group warfare.

'interest/boredom' cues can make a huge difference in group settings and dealing with people who you do not already know.

It also helps a lot to actually be interested in people. Most people have something interesting to say, and asking open questions can help lead to common ground.

Unless you're sure of the company you're with, it's a good idea to avoid dropping into monologues about your current obsession and focus on what you know is common ground, listening at least as much as you are talking. Try to treat it as a game, one where learning new strategies is more important than getting a perfect score.

On the subject of games, a book I found very helpful as an insight into some of the more incomprehensible NT behaviour was *Games People Play*, by Eric Berne, MD. There are lots of books about body language, creating rapport, etc. out there but this one goes in detail into those NT exchanges that happen when relationships appear from the outside to be going a bit wrong – but everyone is actually getting 'payoffs' that they often won't admit even to themselves. Each of these patterns of human transactions, or 'games' as they are called in the book, has a name. I'm sure that some of these games, such as the bully's favourite of 'See What You Made Me Do', will be immediately and painfully familiar to Aspies. The book has a lot to say about how to break out of such games, and avoiding pathological relationships with people who play the unhealthier games.

It was a 'hyper-NT' friend of mine who first told me about this book – this was before I was aware of Asperger syndrome. In retrospect it is obvious that he saw something autistic about me – he even called me by the nickname 'Rain Man' for a short while until he realised I found it very annoying.

One final word of warning – some NTs feel that learning their tricks is 'cheating' at the social game – so if you are trying a bit of social mimicry it's best to keep the fact to yourself.

THE LINK BETWEEN INTERNAL AND EXTERNAL STATES
This is something I am often guilty of overlooking, but when feeling down it is more important than ever to continue to eat healthily, exercise, and keep your general hygiene and surroundings in order. We take it for granted that feeling down can make us feel physically

rotten, but the other side of the mind–body link, that our mental state can be as easily affected by physical changes in our bodily state, is easy to overlook.

When I feel depressed I often lose sight of the fact that I will not feel this way forever, and that there is a bodily component to the feeling that can be dealt with by purely physical means.

As a sometime wannabe 'tragic hero', I sometimes feel silly when I find that the dead weight of existential ennui has been lifted by nothing more than a bracing walk and a cup of tea. Even something as simple as taking a shower can lift some of that 'heavy' feeling and inertia that comes with a blue day.

BREAKING THE CYCLE OF GUILT

I find that depression usually comes served with a generously portioned side-salad of guilt. I find I often feel guilty and depressed about feeling 'behind' in a lot of areas of my life, but feeling depressed keeps me from taking active steps to catch up with everything I feel I need to do, so I feel I am wasting valuable time, which makes me feel guilty, which makes me feel depressed...

It's a vicious circle that I still have difficulty with, and I don't have a complete answer to it, but I have a strategy that at least sometimes keeps it from snowballing out of control. Winston Churchill, who referred to his depression as 'the black dog', said: 'If you are going through hell, keep going.'... and Edmund Burke said: 'Never despair, but if you do, work on in despair.'

When I start persecuting myself for not living up to my expectations, I try to focus on just one small thing that will improve my situation in one small way, and put aside feelings of guilt until I am finished. When I am done I often find the feelings of guilt have subsided, and the resultant feeling of lightness helps me focus on the next item on my list. And if the feelings are still there, I find at least I have enjoyed taking a break from them.

GULLIBILITY, DECEPTION AND HIERARCHIES

People with AS are among the most trusting, honest and open types you will find. Unfortunately, while society pays lip service to the idea that these are admirable qualities, in reality they are generally seen as a sign of weakness to be exploited. I have a theory that deceiving, and detecting the deceptions of others, is the main reason why the NT 'theory of mind' evolved.

I've been stung plenty of times by the lies and deceptions of others, and from what I have read this is a common Aspie experience.

As a child I was easily led and too trusting for my own good, which caused me some problems and taught me some hard lessons. Despite that, I have been deceived and taken advantage of in adult life too. Trusting someone and being badly let down can have a very negative effect on your ability to trust others, which is important for good relationships and mental health, so I think it is good to have a few defensive measures up your sleeve.

My earlier point about studying NT behaviour can be of some help in avoiding being used, ripped off and generally taken for a sucker, as can having a trustworthy NT friend with instincts you can rely on when something has aroused your suspicions but you are not quite sure – it can look a lot like cynicism but there is a lot to be said for good old-fashioned NT 'common sense', and they can pick up on signs and signals that we Aspies are doomed to miss.

In my experience, if you have to ask someone an awkward question and they respond with something like 'Are you calling me a liar?', then alarm bells should immediately be ringing. This is an example of something called 'appeal to authority'. I've never seen this response from someone who is telling the truth and the implicit threat in the question implies they are on the ropes. NTs will use the threat of violence when cornered by evidence if they are on their own. If you corner them when they are with someone else they will attempt to marshal an ally to ridicule you.

Another form of deception is of the 'non-personal' kind and involves people trying to extract money from you, or perhaps just some measure of belief in whatever they're peddling, on dubious grounds. I say it is 'non-personal' because these people effectively 'sweep search' looking for someone who is easily duped. Get-rich-quick schemes, internet scams, miracle cures, etc. all fall under this heading, and scams of this type are everywhere – you will be targeted sooner or later if you have not been already.

There's no infallible way to guard against being taken in in this way, but I would recommend honing your critical faculties, and always questioning claims that appear too good to be true, or simply outlandish. I am a big fan of the scientific method as the best way of coming to the truth of a matter, and there are resources on the internet devoted to developing sceptical, critical rational thought. Other good questions to ask yourself are: 'Is my assessment of whether this is true/false being coloured by the fact that I *want* it to be true/false?'... and 'Who stands to gain the most here?'

The final form of deceit to watch out for is deceit by group consent. NTs love to arrange themselves into rigid and unaccountable hierarchies, possibly a hangover from the days when the 'head of the herd' dictated reproductive rights in the group. This results in a one-way daisy chain of reciprocal oppression called *authority*, and it is something that Aspies commonly have issues with.

I suppose my troubles with authority started as a child, from asking questions when I wasn't supposed to, and asking further questions when given unsatisfying answers, to being accused of lying when I was telling the truth – probably due to the 'eye contact' thing.

When people answer a reasonable question with 'it just is', or something similar, then they are making an appeal to authority (in this case their own authority). When this happens it is a good idea to think about the context you are in and the role of the authority figure. If it is your boss, it may be best to shut up and accept it even when you know you are right. If it is your doctor, then you should take into account that they have years of medical training and that there is an element of validity to their authority *so long as they are speaking on purely medical terms*. If it is someone you consider a friend and they are using the appeal to authority to try and make you do something you don't want to do, then that person may well not be someone you can trust.

It is good to make a mental note of when the appeal to authority happens because it is usually the last step before some more overt form of manipulation, such as use of or threat of the use of force.

Doctors, policemen and other government officials are all figures of authority, and it is a sad fact that people with AS often have more contact with these people than the average Joe. A doctor who can be reasoned with like a human being is like gold dust. The police, in my experience, are just best avoided if at all possible.

All this talk of the dangers of snake-oil merchants and unquestioning group consent brings me neatly onto avoiding the media.

AVOIDING THE MEDIA

The media is a construct created by NTs so they can make each other unhappy and thus extract resources from each other by selling each other products that promise (but fail to) alleviate the resultant unhappiness. Avoid the mainstream media if you can – any information content is incidental – it's there to shift product.

Dealing with the media and finding reliable sources of information in general is a problem that I won't pretend to have solved, but if I was to condense what little I (think I) know into a few quick tips they would be:

- Watching too much TV will make you miserable.

- Watching too much TV *with adverts in* will make you *very* miserable.

- Always consider the motivations of whoever is providing you with information.

- Be careful with newspapers – there is an old quote from a former editor of one of the rags about how one of the prerequisites for a story to be accepted in the paper was that it should leave the reader hating someone or something – these are the newspapers to be avoided.

… 'nuff said.

MEDICATION, THAT'S WHAT YOU NEED

… as Roy Castle used to sing at the end of his show. I think.

There are a lot of people who will deride the taking of pills and claim it is a kind of 'crutch'. My retort to these people is that if they had ever suffered a broken leg they might not be so contemptuous about the usefulness of crutches.

Deciding to use, or not use, medication is entirely your own choice and you should not let other people make you feel guilty about it. Do whatever works for you.

It's your life, and you belong here as much as anyone else.

Chapter 5

A Colourful Rainbow: Embracing Autism as a Neurological Difference, Rather than a Mental Health Disorder

Melanie Smith

Introduction by Luke Beardon

From an individual perspective, Mel provides an exceptionally powerful argument about acceptance; she pushes for parents to accept and embrace who their child is. I would suggest that this argument needs to be taken on board from the wider population, and for the PNT to realise that difference is not synonymous with negativity and that people with AS have as much to offer to society as their PNT peers (if not more).

Mel also makes some good points about myths of autism, and how people should be deterred from making stereotypical assumptions about individuals. As we all know, people with autism/AS are as individual and unique as anyone, and therefore no assumptions should be made. Importantly this concept can be extrapolated to cover how mental health services should respond the individuals — indeed they should do just that, respond to the individual, and their individual need; not all people with AS will respond to support in the same way. The individuality of the population is of paramount importance when providing support.

Autism is spread right across a spectrum called the autistic spectrum. In this spectrum there are different levels of autism and co-morbid neurological 'disorders', all meshed into one colourful rainbow. Or at least that's how I like to think of it.

There is as yet no known cure for autism, and no known cause. Some say it could be caused by mercury in vaccinations. I think that's a load of naïve wishful thinking by parents to make their child become normal. The fact is that your child or someone else's child you know is just plain different. I think parents desperately want a cause for those that are severely autistic and are non-verbal. Yet we praise those that are high-functioning and have extremely special gifts.

The media give fallacious views on autism. There was a woman who killed her autistic child because she loved him so much. When I saw the video, I was so infuriated that other parents felt sympathy and agreed with the woman and daughter as to why she did it. This just shows that there are people out there that will do anything for a cure, or desperately want an answer as to why we have this oddity in human beings. Can't we just accept this 'oddity'? I know I do. I think the world would not be as colourful, if we all followed trends and dressed the same. Albert Einstein was a supposed Aspie, and he is/was legendary.

People with autism are often thought of being severe or an autistic savant, much like the one from the movie *Rain Man* with Tom Cruise and Dustin Hoffman. This misconception is so very clearly wrong. Especially to those who are properly educated on autism and Asperger's. The ones that are best educated on autism, are people that are autistic themselves. I think it's because we know how a 'sensory overload' (and other issues concerning our difference) works and what is best for us to calm it.

Professionals in this field only seem to be knowledgeable about autism, from observing and researching an autistic child. NT (neurotypical/'normal') people seem to be so gullible these days, as to what autism really is. Autism is plain and simple. It is a neurological difference and not a disease. It's not some major disaster to strike an unlucky family. I believe that autism is genetic and not to be caused by something from a toxic chemical. If your child is autistic, deal with it the best way you can, even if it's heartbreaking. The feeling of relief will be worth so much more than that, when you see your child reach a goal they so desperately wanted to achieve.

Today professionals provide some treatments that people actually use. I find this barbaric and it will probably be uncomfortable for their child. The first one I know of is called chelation where they try to remove heavy metals such as mercury from the child's body, to see if it will decompose them of their autism. I think this treatment doesn't even do what it's meant to and just rips families of their money, and cause even more heartache in the process, when they don't see their child improving.

People these days go so far as to creating groups to fight the cause and find a cure for autism. This is just erroneous, we might as well have let Hitler won, from what he so wrongfully believed in; then there wouldn't be any autistic children left, because he would have killed them all. Though I assume the people with AS would have just scraped past their killing.

People are so hell-bent on scoring points from other shallow people that they don't really have time to think of their autistic child and just praise them for their gifts. In other words some people show off their child for all the wrong reasons, and don't think that it will be hurtful or discomforting for their own flesh and blood. In some enigmatic miracle I hope and suspect that my point of view on curbie[1] parents is wrong, and they just want what is best for their children and not themselves. Most parents want sympathy that they're just bringing up some disturbed child and it will make their life a living hell. Three words: Get over it! And get to know and love your child; things will be much happier in the family life if you all just got to know and understand autism and your child.

My view on autism is a positive one and people should try more to embrace their difference more, instead of crying and being heartbroken over it. There is a light at the end of the tunnel and I think people will know that, just by reading my story and seeing who I am today.

I think if I hadn't of been so detached from my feelings and had more empathy — in my situations and to other people, I would have

---

1   'curbie' means believing there is a cure for autism.

ended up in a mental hospital. Now though I have learned how to interact and I can differentiate and recognise my own feelings.

How many of you people reading this, think that autism is people rocking backwards and forwards in straitjackets? Do you think that we don't like being touched, or can't even interpret a meaning that may sound literal? Well if you do, you're so very wrong. Autism is not a mental illness, and we do like to be touched. [Editors' note: Not all people with AS like to be touched, though many do; it is a very individual aspect of AS.] Some of us even have sex and start their own family, either with an NT or an Aspie. An Aspie, Aspie marriage is bound to last longer than Aspie and NT one. [Editors' note: At present there is no evidence to suggest that a partnership between two individuals with AS is more or less likely to last compared to one between an individual with AS and an NT. What is clear is that both can be very successful. This is because they can relate to each other, and don't have to hide who they really are.] We can also learn to uncover the mysteries of body language and any innuendos that may come in a saying or a sentence.

Other mental illnesses, such as depression and schizophrenia, can be parallel or co-morbid with autism, along with things such as fragile-X and Down syndrome. I hope I have clarified enough to help make sure that autism is not a disease or a mental illness. If I haven't that's your own naïve-ness who choose to believe everything a curbie group says because they are so powerful. I'm sorry if I may have been blunt or even mean, but it's just so hard these days, trying to make people understand autism from an autistic point of view.

People in different countries have different theories of how autism works. Some witch-fearing people, believe that autism is because the child is believed to have been possessed by some sort of supernatural force (demon). Are they right or wrong? My answer is wrong! Our brain is just 'wired differently'. I suspect that autism has always been there, right when we were just cavemen. Ever wondered if the lonesome caveman that's making the tools, might be an Aspie? I think they were. Though their brain might have been developing into what the human brain is today.

My point to this babble that I'm writing is to make you see that autism is just a neurological brain difference, and should not be hated by the likes of those who make it their mission to find a cure. If you are autistic or anywhere along the spectrum, try to think of your difference as a gift and not anything hateful. I know I do…

Chapter 6

Getting the Right Diagnosis, and Its Impact on Mental Health: Is This the Best the NHS Can Do?

Cornish

Introduction by Luke Beardon

Cornish's writing can come across as quite bitter and negative towards the PNT world; and quite rightly so. Reading Cornish's 'missive' is a great way to ascertain what one's own levels of empathic understanding might be. When reading it, do you feel yourself thinking 'this guy really does have a chip on his shoulder' – or 'the world really has let this individual down'?

What is so shocking about this chapter is the fact that it could be applied to so many other people with AS who have never been diagnosed or who have had a late diagnosis. Both the lateness of the diagnosis and the struggle to get a diagnosis have had an impact on Cornish, both in a negative way. This is as good an example of writing as any highlighting the dangers of not diagnosing people at an appropriate age, and not supporting an individual through the diagnostic procedure.

In addition to the above there are elements of the writing that demonstrate just how harsh the PNT world can be, and from a very young age. Being bullied – as a child or an adult – we all know to be wrong. We are all aware at how horrific it can be, and some are aware of the potential consequences of it. However, are we all confident in saying that people with AS are no longer bullied? I very much doubt it.

Cornish is understandably reticent about entering into the health service based on his and others' experiences. This is to be appreciated – and the response should be to rectify the wrongs that can be done to people like Cornish, not to ignore them.

Right, here we go again, another missive from the internals of Cornish World, and as the title implies (but not in so many words)... how my local mental health teams did a real 'number' on Cornish, and really screwed me up.

I blame a lot of this on mainstream school. You are indoctrinated from the very start not to question, but to trust blindly, anyone in positions of authority and public power. They are the professionals... you are an ignorant 'grunty farty'... just another member of Joe Public. Don't think for a moment you think you know what's good for you, because according to the people that make the important decisions regarding your well-being... you actually know fuck-all. From teachers to GPs to your local MP, you had better know your place in the grand scheme of it all... after all... they are the ones who have spent all that time in college and uni, put all that effort in to passing those social acceptancy exams (bearing in mind, exams are no indication of competency), started to read the right kind of newspaper and stuck their tongues all the way down the back of the relevant people's pants and become a part of the system that contributes to the right sort of breeding, and in doing so keeps the people segregated... But don't think anyone will be honest enough to own up to this, we wouldn't want to break social convention and start a revolution... no, we will just keep politely complaining and so perpetuate this big illusion that we are all equal. Not only does this cause a great deal of misery, frustration and grief, it can also for a large number of people effectively turn off the 'light at the end of the tunnel'; for many who have put their trust and faith in this so-called professional, it can turn out to be fatal!

Society depends on everyone fitting into the proper designated boxes, and this is never more so when it comes to dealing with mental health. When I started doing some foundational courses covering this topic, it contributed more to my sense of despondency and depression than anything that my past reactive depression ever did. I was horrified and scared out of my wits when I realised the sort of power that is wielded by people once they qualify... I know we are all fallible, but the scope to get things so wrong with so much ease, with no real culpability opened my eyes to why the general public at large will never get to know just what goes on behind the mental health scenes... and in the end, when a diagnosis or treatment boils down to one individual's opinion – it makes me want to catch the next Shuttle flight off-planet. And to put this into simple terms, I am a walking testament of what results when things, like I have just mentioned, go horribly wrong... horribly, horribly wrong.

Okay, we're getting on to personal history here, and if it turns into a bit of a rant, well that's just how it goes, but bear in mind that this is all factual stuff, and probably not unfamiliar to a lot of people reading this... so I'm not making any apologies if I do go off on one.

My mental health problems started way back in August 1963. This was my first day at school, so yes, believe it or not, my reactive depression started when I was four-and-a-half, that's when I started wishing that I would just die... wishing that I'd never been born, crying myself to sleep every night in despair, dreading the coming dawn. Going to school was like being forced into a mental and emotional concentration camp. And so, the only thing I could do, being a passive Aspergian was to withdraw into a world of autistic hell.

I was systematically bullied by teachers and pupils alike for the full 11 years. The hurt and the pain destroyed my small fragile sense of self. By the time I left, I was so traumatised that I had no self-esteem, no sense of self-worth, and no self-confidence and had little or no opinion of myself or anything else that made up the world I existed in. Honest, I look back and I cannot believe how ill I was back then. I tried to tell the people in charge time and time again that things weren't right, but as usual no one was listening, no one wanted to listen. I could only logically conclude that I had lost the power of communication. I was completely lost and alone, I was standing on the brink of a 'total infinity vortex' (see *The Hitchhiker's Guide to the Galaxy*), I had totally lost touch with anything and everything.

The thing that hurts the most now looking back is, 'I can't believe I let them do this to me'. But being only a child, what can you do?

So, on leaving school I was totally 'un-hinged', truly an alien in an alien world, and I had no idea what was going on with me. One thing I have found with Aspergians is, we are very good at running from things, with no clue to where we are running to, and that is exactly what I did... three years in the Royal Navy was a very close-run thing so far as suicide was concerned. I could never have envisioned anything worse than school, but really, 'out of the frying pan into the fire' could not have been more appropriate. My way of thinking at this time just shows the state my mind was in to make such a move. I was in a constant state of depression, despair and always on the brink of suicide, and this, as well as all the usual Aspergian 'qualities', kept me in a state of mental and physical exhaustion.

Whenever I had time to myself, I slept. When I left school, I slept... when I left the Navy, I slept. When I wasn't sleeping, I was trying to work out why I couldn't get a girlfriend, and all of this contributed to my mental anguish.

Fast-forward a couple of years, and Cornish has managed to get wed to a dedicated man-hater. The thing with man-haters is they always need a man around so they can comprehensively punish them. So once again I'm getting a real physical, emotional and mental battering... three years later, I finally get the message and leave.

However, it was during my time of trying to be 'normal' (marriage, job, mortgage, children, car, etc. well, just trying to be me, but getting nowhere fast) that I first came into contact with our local mental health service. My GP had diagnosed me with reactive depression, and had referred me to the psychiatric department of the local hospital, where I was seen by one of these so-called pillars of the community.

As I related all the major problems I had experienced in my life, this total stranger sat opposite me with an air of arrogance that had me thinking that my wife was actually on to something. The doctor was sat on the other side of his desk, in what was very obviously his territory, looking over steepled fingers, in a very smug fashion; I had been explaining about the difficulties I have with change, when he launched into a lecture about how being static in one's thinking leads to stagnation and the putrification of the mind, and then went on to tell me how I had been comprehensively rejected from birth by my parents. He then interrogated me about my relationship with my parents, all the while nodding in a 'I thought so, but I'm keeping this to myself' way, it really was a 'I'm the one who's okay, and you are the one who's fucked – who do you think is in control here?'

Not knowing any better, and because he was, after all, the professional, I took this all on board, and believed every word he said. This was 1980; I was 21, and that meeting had me thinking for the next twenty or so years that it was my parent's fault that I was the way I was. I now know nothing could have been further from the truth.

But it did mean that I practically cut my parents out of my life because of it. And this is what I mean when I say that one person's opinion can cause so much damage in a person's life – I feel I missed out on so much with my parents because of this man.

So here we have a typical example of why the NHS should never be let loose on any Aspergian without specific training and, just as important, visible qualifications. And this brings us on to the mentality and blinkered and out-moded thinking of our illustrious mental health service.

I think most of us on the Aspergian spectrum are very familiar with the chasm that exists between the departments of Learning Disability and Mental Health that we disappear down, but the problem is much more serious than that. What we are up against is NT (neurotypical) social hysteria, and their immense capacity for refusing to see the truth, and of not being able to accept the plain facts of the matter. It seems we Aspergians touch on all the things that make the NTs very uncomfortable in their society. It seems that everything we are by being naturally Aspergian, makes the NTs in general, clinch their bum-cheeks tightly together. We tend to contravene everything that they find acceptable.

We are talking xenophobia in all of its glory, and to exemplify this, we will move on a few more years.

The way that the NHS trains their psychiatric staff, is to normalise the un-normal... 'these people need curing, so go to it'. Make them normal like everyone else at all cost. Mmmm, well after years of various psychiatric investigations, and eight years of counselling sessions by a very nice community psychiatric nurse (CPN), I was no further to being what the NTs would class as being 'normal', and, I didn't want to be 'normal' anyway. But I still wasn't getting any answers. And I was still being asked ridiculous questions like... 'Had I been abused by my parents when I was a child?'

So here we have the childhood trauma approach. Fair enough I suppose, but if you only use this to ascertain problems, you are going to do immense damage, as I can testify. Are all the NTs conditioned to think that any difference in people can be put down to sexual or behavioural abuse in childhood? Has the general public been so indoctrinated by the Freudian perceptions of mental illnesses that if any deviation from their accepted expectations sends them into a frightened state of hysteria? Well yes it does. Don't forget, it's only been 50 years or so, since any sort of deviation was institutionalised.

So it seems beyond the NTs ability to shift their Freudian perceptions to understand neurological disorders. According to the training that psychiatrists receive, the rule is, where the cause is unknown, always look for the physical reason.

Again this way of thinking has been responsible for some grave and unbelievable errors of diagnosis, (mine included), especially in the Freudian years of the 60s, 70s, 80s, right up to the present day. Also, have none of these professionals realised that the Aspergian psyche is obviously going to be a field in its own right? Of course it is.

By definition, because the wiring is so very different, it will need an approach unique to itself! Until the Aspergian psyche is included in the education that these people receive, there will always be blunders, misdiagnoses and pure bafflement, and in the end... fatalities. NT society has to start to take responsibility for why our suicide rate is 6 per cent higher than the national average. Ignorance is no longer a viable excuse.

Anyway... I rant. Let's fast-forward a bit more. The year is 2001. This year was my total *annus horribilis*. Things in my life could not have gone any worse, and I was mentally 'coming apart at the seams'.

My years of seeing my CPN, had seen little benefit for me. Although he was a kind and gentle man, what I saw was his other clients were getting well, and I wasn't. This just exacerbated my depression further. Why were others getting better, and not me? No answers, never any answers that I could find to give me peace of mind. He was coming up to retirement, the local primary care trust (PCT) had re-shuffled the mental health teams and I would no longer receive on-going counselling treatment… when he went… I was basically fucked… he was my only support at that time.

However, a revelation was on the horizon. An acquaintance of mine had been talking to a psychologist friend of his, and on describing my condition, his friend had said 'That doesn't sound like it's just depression… it sounds more like Asperger syndrome.'… Well fuck me, miracles do happen!

After I'd been told, I looked it up on the internet, and would you believe it, there I was being described in absolute detail. I had the answers that I'd been looking for. I'd been searching the whole of my life, and here at last, everything I'd been trying to explain to everybody was there in black-and-white. And better still… it was an official diagnosis. Now people would have to listen to me. Now I could get the correct diagnosis, get correct treatment for it, obtain understanding off the professionals and my life would turn into a bed of roses… how fucking wrong was I?

I informed my CPN of this, he said that it wasn't something he had come across before, but it sounded about right, and was up for taking it to my consultant for verification. So off we went to see the consultant, who I think had a thing against patients diagnosing themselves, and was very unhelpful. This just forced me into an even blacker mood, and when my CPN retired a week later, I thought that it would be better to just end it all. But having said that, as usual, all I really wanted was the pain to stop…

I was hanging on to life by my fingernails. And this is where it gets incredible.

Things were so bad by now that I'd actually started to put my affairs in order. Enough was enough. This imbecile of a psychiatrist was destroying my last hope of life… so near, and yet so far away. He wouldn't even entertain the thought of Asperger syndrome. He printed some leaflets off, and sent me away with a proverbial flea in my ear... and I felt utterly crushed. At my next appointment, I informed him that I intended to commit suicide within the next couple of weeks, and he said: 'Make another appointment – I'm going away on holiday for eight weeks.'... I couldn't believe it, had he not listened to a word I'd said? Obviously not! Again I was under the impression that I'd lost the power of communication, and was lost in a weird mental no-man's land.

Four months later, and I'm in a psyche ward. I look back and feel that this was criminal. I'd lost it completely, and my GP had 'booked' me in. Things 'inside' weren't that much better, and believe me... you couldn't tell the staff from the patients. No one came to talk to me, no one gave me any support and no one gave me any hope. All they did was make sure we ate, and went to bed on time and took our meds. But it did give me a break from the daily grind and get my mental breath back. So my experiences of the psychiatric ward was one of being in a holding facility, and not a warm caring environment... Oh, and while we're at it, no one had even heard of Asperger syndrome, so I felt even more alone.

After a fortnight, I'd had enough of realising that this wasn't the answer to my problems. The way the NHS goes about dealing with mental health meant that there was no way there was going to be a rescue for me, no Seventh Aspergian Cavalry coming over the hill. So I wangled my way out, and went home. I'd talked to some of the auxiliary staff about AS, and they had pointed out that the expertise that I needed didn't exist within the county, and that if I thought that the PCT would fund out-of-county input specifically for my needs, then I'd be waiting forever – it took a while to get my head round this... but this is the world of the NT don't forget. It wasn't ever going to happen.

On leaving the ward, I was in a bit of a no-man's land with not having a diagnosis. I had previously changed my GP to a more sympathetic one, and at my next appointment with him I said: 'Right, I don't want to spend any more time on a psyche ward so let's stop pissing about and get me a diagnosis sorted out.'

So he got in touch with a specialist psychiatrist, who according to my GP would diagnose me. Okay, things were looking up.

'I'll put in for funding from the PCT,' he informed me. Great, my mental health took a shot in the arm. A few weeks later he informed me that the PCT wouldn't have anything to do with it, and had flatly refused the funding. My mental health took an immediate nose-dive!

Okay... so that's how the NTs want to play it! In that case I'll go private. In that moment, I realised that, literally, the only person that was going to administer any sort of treatment, support or otherwise, was going to be myself. There was no understanding of the Aspergian genotype within the NHS or government authorities... zilch, nada, nothing... so, Cornish, don't expect any... not for the next 50 years anyway. Cornish's mood takes an up-turn. We're going to self-empower.

From then onwards, I read and researched everything there is to know about the Aspergian genotype. It became my all-time consuming specialist obsession. It did for me, what no one else has been able to... it filled in all of the blanks. It gave me all the answers that I'd been desperately looking for.

It also confirmed to me that the road I'd taken Cornish down had been the right one. In forsaking the NT world quite early on in life, I'd saved myself more stress and grief than I could have imagined. After marriage, I'd opted out. I don't think I would still be here if I hadn't.

Come 9th of June 2003, I'd gone private, and after borrowing the finances, I was diagnosed... no thanks to the PCT.

My experiences with the NHS ruled out any future involvement with them. I could never trust them with my well-being ever again. There was no chance I was going to allow them anywhere near me again. I simply didn't have time for the ignorance and scepticism displayed by the professionals within the local authorities. They did not like the fact that I was an expert on something that they should know about... but didn't. So instead of trying to understand something entirely unique to the planet, they choose instead to display arrogance and belligerence. You can't work with that. So I chose not to... so fuck 'em.

For the first time in my life, I was too valuable to let the likes of them loose on me. Whatever conditioning I'd received at school to respect authority, disappeared up its own arse, never to appear again. They have had their chance, they've blown it big time!

However, I still had a lot of unresolved issues from my past. Stuff from school especially. Stuff from the Navy. A lot of trauma had been stored up over the years, and needed sorting. I got lucky. There was an autism charity not too far from where I lived, and working there was an Aspergian-specific counsellor, she was private, with no attachment to the NHS. I'm not religious… but what a godsend. Just not having to justify my way of being, my existence, was a unique experience in itself. Having someone who didn't need everything explaining to them was a breath of fresh air. Just having someone who completely understood everything about me was a relief that I can't put into words… just being accepted for who I am made all the difference – Jan I'm forever in your debt.

It took two years of intensive therapy with Jan to undo all the damage that occurred at the hands of the NHS psychiatric staff, and how to forgive them too. It all went very well, and my life has never been better. Oh… and by the way, the PCT never funded one session with Jan, despite numerous referrals from my GP. They still have no interest in taking responsibility for adult Aspergians… thanks for that… not!

In the final analysis, my advice for any fellow Aspergian would be: Don't get involved with the NHS when it comes to mental health issues. There is lots of anecdotal evidence that backs up my experiences. It is essential that you track down the right specialists, no matter how long it takes, no matter how much it costs and no matter how far you have to travel.

Do anything less, and you will be storing up future trouble for yourself and your family. Believe me, unless these people have an Aspergian in the family, they will know sweet FA about you, and won't particularly care. So don't take the chance.

Never forget this is your life they are screwing around with… and never forget:

[the people with the best intentions… can do the most damage…]

Groove on, fellow Aspergians! – Cornish x

Chapter 7

Positive Mental Attitude: Coping with Setbacks, Knowing Your Own Strengths, and Finding Happiness Any Way You Can

Dean Worton

Introduction by Luke Beardon

Dean is an exceptionally bright individual whose work ethic and general morality are of the highest standards. That he has not been appreciated by others, including employers, in the past is disgraceful.

Dean provides some very sensible advice for helping to reduce possible problems with mental health. His advice has been generated though his own experience and, thus, will not be applicable to every person with AS. However, the basis for his suggestions are sound and make an awful lot of sense.

In particular I found the imagery of using a box to keep emotions in particularly poignant and, potentially, of great use to some people. His discussion of bullying and how one might respond is a refreshingly simple but effective way of a possible pathway for a person who has undergone similar experiences (with or without AS, I suspect).

As Dean notes, he does not often speak up – but when he does, he is always worth listening to.

Introduction

I would say that despite a lot of knock-backs in my adult life, I have managed to stay sane and come out of the other end with a fairly normal life. At school, I never felt that I fitted in and yes it did make me feel left out and I probably was a bit upset that I never seemed to be fully accepted by my peers; and outside school hours I rarely met up with other pupils or with neighbourhood children, yet on the whole I just 'got on' with it. At school, I would get my head down and get on with my work. At home, if I wasn't meeting up with my peers, I felt a bit jealous that they were meeting up with each other and having fun, but I never dwelt on it, and it gave me more time to complete my homework. I liked my own company as I didn't fall out with myself that often. Another thing I used to spend my time doing was drawing imaginary high school timetables. I knew that it probably wasn't going to help me to form friendships as I spent many hours doing this instead of making the effort to get into social situations, however it was an activity which stopped me from thinking about things that were not happening in my life. I found it a strangely therapeutic activity, maybe because creating a timetable is a problem-solving task and it is said that spending time on puzzles keeps our minds active. I guess if our minds are active, we are less likely to have negative thoughts.

After leaving school, I struggled to reach the necessary level to go to university and it did get me down a bit that most of my classmates were a few years younger than me and those who were the same age had already worked. When I finally started university, I was 22 years old. I was expecting there to be some mature students on the course but I was the oldest bar one. Most students were 18 and even the 19-year-olds had already taken a year out and worked. I did feel a bit down that I seemed to have done so much less with my life than everyone else but again didn't dwell on it. At the end of the day, I was there to study towards a degree, which is just what I did. I did have friends at first but somehow lost them during the first year having clearly offended them but not feeling that the one or two mistakes I knew I had made were enough to end a friendship over if the friendship meant anything. Only years later, did I remember an incident which was a more plausible explanation, yet at the time I couldn't understand what had gone wrong and felt quite alone in this big city that I had moved into to study my degree. This was coupled with financial problems that I was having at the time. It was a struggle to pay rent, bills and food and not a particularly pleasant experience.

Great life experience

My German class were all going to Leipzig at the beginning of September to take an intensive course in German. I desperately wanted to go and took on a job as a checkout operator in order to fund it, but this didn't work out. The only way I would be able to continue paying my rent and also go to Leipzig would have been to get another part-time job. I did find another part-time job but it didn't pay enough to allow me to go to Leipzig. I was hoping to be able to borrow the money to go to Leipzig, but this was not possible. I spent the next one or two weeks feeling very depressed as I wanted to go to Leipzig so much and if I didn't go I would be literally the only person in my German class not to be able to go. It was the summer holidays and I had stayed in my shared accommodation many miles away from home in order to do my part-time job but this was just in the evenings, and the only college work I was able to do was studying all of my German workbooks, which of course was rather depressing as this only reminded me that I might not be going to Leipzig. Therefore for about a fortnight, I spent several hours in my flat I think trying to have extra sleep as I couldn't think of another way to avoid thinking of this horrible predicament. Its one of the worst feelings I've ever experienced. Luckily as it turned out my access to money wasn't as tight as I thought and I was able to get an extension on my student overdraft sooner than I thought and this allowed me to go to Leipzig.

Leipzig was a fantastic experience for me despite being required to spend the two weeks in a flat with a German teenager, who I had never met before and go to classes taken by ladies who never spoke any English to us the whole time we were there and having to travel sometimes alone from one side of Leipzig to the other. I am very confident at travelling alone on my own and being abroad or visiting anywhere at all is something which does wonders for my mental health. For example, whenever I have some time alone in London,

I will get a bus or underground train to a random place and wander around aimlessly feeling awestruck at what is around each corner and having a wide smile on my face throughout the experience because I feel so free and am always fascinated by witnessing how other people live their lives and the historical story behind why an object can be found on a random street corner. In life in general, exploring new places and things is the way that I cope in times of stress or if I'm worried about something. I've always tried to keep a positive mental attitude in the face of adversity. Naturally, some of the things people do to take their mind off things might actually remind them of the very thing that they are trying to take their mind off, although if I'm trying to take my mind off something that hasn't worked out, I try to remain emotionally detached in that situation and not think about the connection. Usually this is not too difficult. No matter how bad things get there are usually people worse off and if I do go through a period of being down about something, I know that this won't be for ever.

Setbacks

Some setbacks have seemed to be quite far-reaching and no amount of soul searching seemed to be able to remedy that. For example, I was 26 by the time I finished my degree. I returned to my home town and looked for work. By chance, a company in a city 50 miles away was looking for Language Assistants. I applied for this, and had I been appointed would have had the opportunity to use my main foreign language, French. I almost missed out on the interview because I was out when they called, and when I called back they seemed reluctant to keep the interview offer open. However, an interview was arranged and although I set off, due to bad planning before setting off I was unable to make it to the premises. I applied again when they had further positions, but it seemed that my fate was sealed. There was a big firm just five miles from home that needed French speakers. I applied there three times, but couldn't get in due to the nature of the other skills needed. In the end, the closest I came to working with languages was working for seven months in a translating company and helping out with translating documents from time to time and while I was pleased to be working in a firm which dealt with foreign languages, I was mainly doing administration in my own language and feeling envious that others in the same office were using languages. I have to admit that not getting to that interview when I was 26 is one of my biggest regrets. I do take some solace in the fact that I might have never been appointed anyway or I might have been appointed but not lasted due to Asperger traits interfering but having not disclosed because this was prior to knowing about Asperger's. The thing is though I just don't know and never will.

At first, I was depressed about this. Although I found alternative employment, it was bitty and didn't make use of my university education and it did come back to haunt me occasionally. However, we all have regrets and we mustn't allow them to take over our lives. Some things are just not meant to be, and we need to keep a positive frame of mind. Not having a job and being short of money is not pleasant and too many people with Asperger syndrome are struggling in the job market because employers are using ambiguous terms in their recruitment campaign which are offputting to people with Asperger syndrome who simply want to have a job. However, I think it's time for us to be realistic about the world we are all living in. It is not created for people with Asperger syndrome, it is created for NTs. This however does not mean that we have any less right to be happy than anyone else. I believe firmly in finding happiness any way you can. It may be that the nature of someone's AS restricts them from finding happiness from the same source as the majority of people. However, if you can't tap into the same experiences that NTs can, let's say because you couldn't strike up a conversation with a stranger at a party, so you end up being the only person sitting there mute, this does not make you a less valid individual so don't go to parties thinking that you must approach other people and then beating yourself up for not being able to. Whatever situation you're in as long as you're not harming others or yourself, just be yourself, you have every right to be the person that you are and you have a lot of good qualities. Personally, I have no problem if I'm with a group of people and not doing much speaking and I also know that anything I did say would be worthwhile.

Advice to others

DAILY ROUTINE

In order to achieve good mental health, I would recommend to anyone that they develop a good daily routine. This doesn't mean being obsessive about doing the same thing at the same time every day. It simply means having a rhythm in your life. I remember at times when there was nothing specific to get up for I used to go to bed late and get up late and be told that I should be in bed by 11pm and get up at 9am. At the time, I couldn't understand what difference it made if I was getting the same amount of sleep anyway. However in practice, I find that it feels far more natural going to bed before 11pm and get up at around 7.30am and since adopting the routine of going to bed and getting up at these times, I think my mental health has improved greatly.

I would also recommend to anyone that they try to do some sort of rigorous exercise every morning and evening. If you don't do anything else, you could try doing twenty sit ups in the morning and twenty sit ups in the evening. The evening sit ups give you some energy before you even get up in the morning although you need to do them more than an hour before bed otherwise you'll struggle to get to sleep. The morning sit ups give you energy for whatever you do with the day. You can gradually increase to thirty sit ups a time and for special events when you need more energy, you could do an extra lot of sit ups for that extra bit of energy. All this helps to get the blood flowing more smoothly which makes you feel better. In my opinion, the better you feel physically the better you feel mentally.

Try not to be put off by what others who live with you will say. If it's gentle teasing, you may feel initially embarrassed but you can overcome this. Our mental health should never be allowed to suffer due to fear of ridicule. If someone would be overbearing in their ridicule then try to find somewhere more private to do your exercises with the curtains closed such as your bedroom. If you have no audience then no one will think you silly. In fact if you put some music on behind closed doors you might even decide to have a bit of a dance to the music. If no one can see what you're doing who cares? Of course, if you can get a room with a television and a bit of spare space to yourself why not use an exercise video?

OVERCOMING BARRIERS

I know some people will be reading this and thinking that all this sounds ridiculous, but if good mental health is going to be achieved, I think that those negative thoughts need putting away in a box somewhere (not literally). You need to be willing to try things and not give up the first time it doesn't work out because no one gets everything right the first time. If I had given up anything that didn't quite work out the first time I tried it, I might be sitting at home wondering what had happened to my life. I think that everyone has a good life waiting for them, but that they have to take some disappointment before things start to go their way. I'm sure you can think of some successful people who didn't start out very lucky. If they hadn't kept on getting back up and trying again or taking a different approach, some of the world's greatest creations which make life better might not be here for us all to enjoy. I think that life is what you make it. Naturally, if you have had a genuinely bad experience, it would require a great deal of determination to reduce the negative thoughts that this causes but there are indeed people who have had horrible things happen to them who pull through and make a great life for themselves.

CONTROLLING YOUR OWN SELF-ESTEEM

If you've experienced a lot of bullying in your life, then consider this analogy. If you haven't experienced any, substitute the bully with an unpleasant situation.

You feel good about yourself when along comes a bully who decides to make your life as unpleasant as they can. They have an invisible implement and they keep chipping away at your heart with this implement. They have an imaginary box that they carry around with them and every time they meet you they remove a tiny part of your heart or soul. This part of your heart or soul is your self-esteem. Eventually they have taken away all or most of your self-esteem. If you continue to meet this person they will continue to carry this box around with them. If you stop meeting them or if they start to torment someone else instead, they will no longer carry this box around with them all the time. If they apologise for what they have done then they are presenting you with the imaginary box. Your self-esteem is inside that box so you have a choice about whether to keep the lid of the box closed and leave all the pain locked inside the box or be brave enough to unlock the box and take back your self-esteem. If the bully never apologies but stops tormenting you they won't be carrying this box around. They have abandoned the box somewhere and it's for you to find the box before they retrieve it again and start chipping away at your self-esteem again. It might take a while to find the box but with the right amount of determination you can find the box and take back your self-esteem.

If the bully took away a lot of your self-esteem, then the contents of the box will be heavy and you may be unable to retrieve the contents in one go. It will probably take time to get back all of your self-esteem if someone has taken it away from you, but if you don't allow anyone else to take the box off you, then there is always self-esteem waiting in that box that you are carrying around with you to dip into in order to gain more self-esteem. If you've never done anything deliberately to harm anyone else then you are a good person and the person who took away your self-esteem in the first place had no right to. More often than not, people who steal other people's self-esteem are probably just trying to replace self-esteem that they themselves are missing. After all, how can someone genuinely feel good about themselves if they are bullying someone?

Don't ever let anyone else carry your self-esteem around for you; always make sure that you are in control of and carrying around your own self-esteem. No matter what difficulties you suffer in this world not designed for people with Asperger syndrome, you are who you are, you have every right to be the person that you are (as long as you're not harming anyone) and you should feel happy and proud being the person that you are. No matter how hard life becomes make the very best of it that you can, and should any opportunity ever be closed to you as a result of your Asperger syndrome and no amount of fighting against it will help (although it might), then simply find another opportunity that isn't closed to you.

Don't assume that just because you are living with Asperger syndrome that opportunities open to you will be limited. I'm sure that each and every Aspie reading this book has the potential to tap into opportunities that some neurotypicals will envy them for. Above all, don't forget that Aspies can often think in unique and useful ways that few neurotypicals can. This does not mean that neurotypicals are less intelligent or that Aspies are more intelligent, but many Aspies who have thought in a positive way have tapped into inner resources that neurotypicals are perhaps less likely to, despite being equally able.

Perhaps one day, you will have taken all of your self-esteem out of the box. If this happens you will no longer be carrying the box around with you. There is a piece of string attached to the box. The bully yanked hold of the piece of string when he carried the box around so that he could be in control of your self-esteem but when you have taken back of all your self-esteem, the box will not stay in position as it was relying on the contents to keep it weighted down. As soon as the box becomes empty, it will be tugged by this piece of string into some empty void where you don't have to carry it around with you but as soon as you lose any self-esteem the box will snap into its previous position. This box is heavy and you don't want to carry it around with you, so do whatever you can to make the box as light as possible. No one who takes your self-esteem away from you is better than you and no matter what anyone says to make you feel bad about yourself, no one ever has the right to bully anyone else.

DIET AND EXERCISE

A healthy diet can improve mental health even if this means being open to trying some foods you have disliked up until now. Ideally you should have a healthy snack mid-morning and mid-afternoon such as crackers in the morning and a piece of fruit in the afternoon.

Getting the right amount of exercise is a great source of mental well-being. If sit ups, press ups or exercise videos are not for you and you're not sure about going out for a jog even though it's food for thought, you might want to think about joining a gym. I'm not sure about elsewhere in the world, but in the UK most leisure centres have a gym where all you pay for is your induction and your session so that you are not compelled to keep going in order to get your money's worth. The gym is not for everyone and this is only a suggestion. However, don't allow self-consciousness or low self-esteem to stop you going. Again, if you don't feel good about yourself then take some self-esteem out of the imaginary box.

SELF-HELP BOOKS

In my late twenties, I read a book on how to improve your confidence in seven days. About a month later, I was on a three-day training course. For the first one and a half days, I didn't say much. I got gradually more and more self-conscious of the fact that I wasn't really contributing anything. In the afternoon of the second day, we were put into groups to try to solve a problem. I have always tried to make my point of view known in small group situations and am eager that no one should report back to the rest of the class that I didn't speak. I haven't always found it particularly easy to make my voice heard in situations where everyone is trying to speak, but somehow on this occasion, I got my voice heard and everyone seemed to respect what I was trying to say. Suddenly, I was on a roll and when there needed to be a group spokesperson at the end, without hesitation I volunteered and in similar situations since then the same has happened. I clearly had leadership skills that I had never before had the courage to tap into and some of my previous bad experiences could easily have prevented me from having the confidence to ever do anything towards discovering this potential.

KNOWING YOUR STRENGTHS

I think the key to good mental health is never to give up. Most cars that we see are being driven by people who didn't give up at the first or even second hurdle, and how often does someone get a basketball through the hoop the first or second time they try? Not many! My twenties were rife with setbacks to living a normal and happy life but now in my thirties, I'm running my own flat and after just eight cooking lessons can make myself some nice healthy and nutritious meals and I have a full-time job which involves regular contact with several senior managers. I'm not the most confident of communicators, preferring e-mails to the telephone. Unlike my colleagues, I never make smalltalk with any of the managers and maybe to some seem quite serious and a bit cold, but I get the information I need from them without being rude or unpleasant and my manager says that I have a good rapport with the managers. A few years ago, I thought that I might go through life doing dead-end jobs that don't make use of my degree yet through doing a lot of voluntary work to bring my skills up to speed and realising my capabilities, I am now doing a reasonably paid job with a bit of responsibility where I am valued.

The absolute most important thing is that we are all the way we were made and we need to accept this and appreciate ourselves for the person that we were made. Remember, that everyone is here for a reason, and everyone has something unique to offer to the world whether Aspie, NT or even any other disability. Never judge yourself by your disability and even if you declare yourself as having a disability for official purposes, try not to think of yourself as disabled. Just think of the official disclosure procedure as something you have to do to educate people who are uneducated people about your 'difference'. Instead of thinking 'why should you have to do this when others don't?' just grin and bear it. I find it so much better just to get on with these procedures and not think about it too much. It can be helpful to open up with employers and suchlike about how Asperger's affects you. While mentioning the things you do struggle with, place more emphasis on your positive points. If you see yourself as a disabled person, you are more likely to be treated like one.

It's understandable that many Aspies feel bad about themselves when they are apparently taken less seriously than everyone else. What you need to start thinking is that you simply think 'differently' to most people and that they are just not educated enough yet to realise this. Always remember that as long as no one is getting hurt, there is not one right and one wrong way to be.

The chances are that you are able to offer something exceptional to someone in the world. As an Aspie, your thinking style is different from the NT majority. Thinking in an unusual way is a blessing and not a curse. Many of the world's greatest writers and musicians were thought to have Asperger traits and their work is celebrated worldwide.

Therapeutic activity

Walking is an activity that I find very enjoyable and would recommend to anybody. It can really clear the mind. I joined a walking group a few months ago in order to get to know other people in my area. The first time I went was on an evening riverside walk. It was August, so still light. It made such a welcome change from being cooped up in my flat in the evening, which happens invariably on weekdays. We stumbled upon a creek where boats were bobbing up and down in the water as though it had been that way for over a hundred years. I find that seeing unexpected sights while on a walk be it in the countryside or a big city can be very interesting because you see life from so many angles. There are many things that I would like to do in life, and I suppose having my own boat and sitting in it looking out at a peaceful river is one of many things I could do that I only really seem to ever observe, as I suppose I'm more of a passive person than an active person. Although I'm proactive about doing things that I've been asked to do or in helping people in some way, when it comes to leisure activities there are not many things that I actively pursue or at least that's what I sometimes think, although not everyone climbs mountains like I do and I feel pretty good about myself when I'm doing this and it wipes away all my stresses through feeling the breeze and enjoying the beautiful views. The second walk was near Kirkby Lonsdale at around the point where Cumbria, Lancashire and Yorkshire all meet up.

One thing I found about the group was that people don't seem to welcome you with open arms, but as you might know by now, I'm not one for giving in so easily. There were about thirty people on the second walk so I could easily have gone unnoticed. However, there was a new member there that day who started talking to me. As I don't drive, we exchanged mobile phone numbers. The next week, he texted me to say he was unable to go walking that weekend. The next thing I knew he rung me up and ask if I wanted to meet for drinks that night. Neither one of us has yet returned to the walking group although we do intend to go again if there is a short walk within our immediate area. However, we have met most weekends in the last few months and gone for a short two- to three-hour walk. If the weather has not been up to it, we have instead gone to watch a film. I want to return to the walking group at some point, but there is no rush as I've already made one friend from it.

Wherever possible, I also walk home at the end of the working day. This takes 40 minutes which is just about right for gaining some benefit from it without it being so long that I can't really be bothered. Having at least one 40-minute walk a day is a good way of keeping fit and reducing stress. Needless to say, there are some days when I do still get the bus, either due to nasty weather or feeling utterly exhausted but otherwise even if I feel slightly tired, I make a point of getting to the street with the bus stop and walking straight ahead without turning into it. With that one act, it's easy to walk home. After eight hours of sitting behind a desk it's a nice feeling to feel the fresh air and so much more liberating than being on the bus. I enter my flat after my 40-minute walk and don't feel nearly as tired as I would if I'd caught the bus and I feel less physically and mentally drained when I get home and washing the pots or filling the washing machine aren't so depressing.

Chapter 8

'It's All in Your Head': The Dangers of Misdiagnosis

Neil Shepherd

Introduction by Luke Beardon

Neil has an enviable writing style and produces articulate and intelligent writing on areas that are often difficult to approach. One thing that struck me on reading this article was the disparity of perception that Neil alludes to on more than one occasion, which potentially is of huge importance, in particular for clinicians working in the field of mental health. There are too many aspects of this paper to comment on, so I will focus simply on one – that of the problems arising for people with AS when clinicians do not understand (or accept) that what appears apparent to them as clinicians from their own perspective may not be an accurate reflection of neurological processing. Take Neil's example of 'hearing voices' – followed by his reflection on what is actually occurring within his brain. This is clearly not an example of psychosis, nor is it related to signs of schizophrenia – and yet how many clinicians would jump straight to that conclusion?

When a clinician meets a person with AS I presume that most of them will assess the presentation of that person and ascertain whether or not they fit criteria for various different mental health issues or problems – and if there are enough similarities then a diagnosis may be made. I am sure this oversimplifies the process, but I suspect the basics are reasonably accurate. What I would argue is the main concern here is that many clinicians will not address the fact

*that they are confronted by a person with AS – and that, as a result, the same
assumptions should not be made as if the individual was neurotypical; indeed,
the presentation of a person with AS may well simply be just that – a person with
AS – not a person who is diagnosable as mentally ill. The characteristics 'seen'
by the clinician might stem directly from the nature of AS and have nothing to
do with mental ill health – Neil's voices in the head are an excellent example
of this. Often, the clinician will see the individual following (or during) times
of great duress, which may compound the issue; nonetheless, it is essential that
clinicians are provided with the appropriate training and support in order to
differentiate better between the nature of AS and mental illness – otherwise it is
highly likely that misdiagnoses will continue to blight the lives of individuals
with AS who may require support – but are not mentally ill.*

Introduction

Can I be honest? Well tough, I'm going to be. When I was asked to
write an article on Asperger syndrome (AS) and mental health I was
more than a little perturbed. I was a little bit annoyed not only by the
implication that I have mental health problems (Skewed perspective
on life? Yes. Twisted sense of humour? Yes. Clinically insane mad
man? No… well, not all the time anyway) but also by the potential
implication that AS and mental health problems go hand in hand and
are, in some way, linked. So I turned it down, reasoning that I simply
didn't have enough experience to write something worthwhile. I
was also scared about treating what is a very 'sensitive' area either
flippantly (as if) or portraying it in the wrong light.

Sadly, as is so often the case, the seed had been sown and while
'conscious me' got on with putting my DVD collection into alphabetical
order (sub-collated by genre and case design of course) 'subconscious
me' (the bit that does the actual thinking and, generally, keeps me on
the straight and narrow) pondered and questioned – it does this and
then, in simplistic terms, sends a text message to 'conscious me' saying
that it's just solved the problems of the universe (I'm pretty sure I'll end
up reading this article back to myself and not have the faintest memory
of writing half of it. Such is the 'problem' of having a 'subconscious
me').

What I realised was that I had all too easily adopted the stereotypical perception (or *mis*-perception) of mental health being limited to conditions such as schizophrenia, Alzheimer's, dementia, etc. (and that all 'mad' people were like 'Howlin Mad' Murdoch from The A-Team). For someone who's always wanting others to look beyond the stereotype and to make their own decisions/conclusions this was somewhat hypocritical. Okay, back to the drawing board and let's look at this 'mental health' thing again… maybe there's something in it that I've missed.

Building the box

The common perception of mental health problems (i.e. the image that springs to mind when the subject is mentioned) is typically that of wild-haired 'crazies' shouting at invisible people, straitjackets, rubber-walled cells and electro-shock therapy (or is that just me?). This is fine as they are all mental health problems (or are all aspects of mental health 'treatment' – even if some of them do come from an almost Dickensian vision of merry olde Englande). What I, and indeed many people, assume is that madness equals mental health problems. It does (from a certain perspective) but mental health problems do *not* equal madness. I needed to look outside of the 'madness box' and consider the mental health 'umbrella' and the conditions that this encompasses (in the same way as the autistic spectrum disorder 'umbrella' is something of a catch-all statement for a wide range of autistic conditions). The big one, and the one that is very often ignored by non-medical types, is that of depression. Then there's a wealth of other conditions that, according to the NHS, fall into the mental health category: alcoholism, panic attacks, OCD, Munchausen syndrome, migraine, etc. Some of these I find 'questionable' (I suffer from migraine and would never have called it a mental health problem – neurological problem yes, but certainly not a mental health problem).

When looked at in this way I realised that I did have some experience in this field and maybe I did have something that I could write about. I've suffered from depression (many times as I will probably detail later on), I've suffered from paranoia (although that was justified, everyone really *did* hate me) and, I have even had voices in my head. (I've since rationalised that this was some kind of 'inner voice' or 'conscience' rather than God, Napoleon or Sean Connery – if it was God then he/she/it spoke with a northern accent and swore a lot. The same goes for Napoleon – Sean Connery I'm not so sure about – I bet he swears like a docker.) This new 'definition' of mental health problems made the possibility of my writing this article switch from being a straight 'no' to a 'maybe' (and the fact that I'm writing it and you're reading it kind of implies that it eventually ended up as a 'yes' – or maybe I went back to saying 'no' and you're imagining the whole thing – if so, could you e-mail me the ending please, I'd love to know what happens).

Mental health and AS

Mental health is a very large and all-encompassing term, but it's not a term that I consider AS to fall under. This is something that I want to stress vigourously: AS is a neurological/developmental condition, it's not 'madness' (mental health can, more often than not, be treated and cured – AS can't be as it's a totally different condition affecting a totally different aspect of the brain in a totally different way). Many people, typically the uninformed (and generally unclean), can't see a distinction, and the treatment of AS and autistic spectrum disorders (ASDs) in the past indicates that this perception and lack of distinction also extended to the medical profession – a situation that has, thankfully, changed considerably (I do often wonder if, born 50 years earlier, I'd have been fitted for a straitjacket and left to rock back and forth in the corner).

Somewhere in the pit of useless knowledge that is my brain a little flag popped up when I was pondering this article and reminded me that the level of mental health problems in the UK is considerably higher than many people think (it's something like one in four or one in five people will suffer from a mental health condition at some time in their life. There's something to fill in the hours of an evening – after reading this meandering collection of half-truths, misconceptions and half-baked ideas, go away and try to find out. That's for later, for now though, back to matter in hand...) This higher-than-expected level of mental health problems is across the population as a whole though so it's only natural that a percentage of Aspergics will also suffer from mental health problems. Is the percentage higher? Maybe yes, maybe no (what do I look like, some sort of statistician – might make an interesting research subject for someone (you can have that idea for free if you're looking for a research project by the way)). In terms of sheer numbers though, an element of Aspergics *will* suffer from mental health problems.

Patient in waiting?

With my Aspergic view of the world, things, events and situations are often seen in a different light (I am Aspergic by the way and I don't think I've stated that in this article yet. In fact I'm totally forgetting my manners – Hello, my name's Neil, sorry I didn't introduce myself earlier on. How are you? Is Roger still doing well at prep school? Did Portia do well at the gymkhana? We really must do afternoon tea more often and etc.). As I've said above, I don't know whether a higher percentage of Aspergics suffer from mental health problems, but I can all too easily see how they might do as I've been there, I've done that and I have an understanding (through first hand experience) of the issues and problems that Aspergics face in this experience we call 'life'.

Why Aspergics may be more susceptible to mental health problems could be for one of two reasons, either a physiological one or psychological one – or, more probably, a combination of the two. Given the developmental issues regarding the autistic brain, there could very well be a 'hardware' predisposition towards mental health problems. I can understand this because, as I often explain it, certain elements of the brain are wired up 'incorrectly' (or 'differently' if you find the term 'incorrect' offensive), underdeveloped (you can think of them as being 'child-like' if you want to but I'm of the opinion that, in some areas, I'm not child-*like*, I am *actually* a child) or simply missing altogether. It stands to reason that if elements of the brain are missing or underdeveloped, dealing with certain elements of 'life' can be impossible, and this can either cause a total blackout (in terms of functionality as opposed to a 'Huh? What just happened?' kind of blackout) or an increased load on other areas of the brain/personality.

This ties in very neatly with the argument that it could be down to a psychological problem (i.e. situation, environment, etc.). Aspergics, like all autistics and any 'disabled' people, have to deal with a world that isn't designed for them. This can cause additional stress, pressure and anxiety as even performing 'simple' tasks can reach a whole new level of difficulty above and beyond what the majority can ever hope to understand. If, as in the Aspergic brain, there is also a physiological 'weakness' in certain areas of the brain, these stressful events, situations, etc. *will* cause an overload, highlight weaknesses, etc.

I'm not saying that all Apsergics are about to flip out, wear pink fluffy slippers to go to Marks and Spencers, or suddenly believe that the Earth is ruled by giant lizard monsters from another dimension, but the inherent differences that make someone Aspergic may very well leave them vulnerable to depression, paranoia, etc. but not, in my opinion, 'classic' mental health problems.

A product of situation

Asperger syndrome is, as is widely known in AS circles, a condition that affects communication, interpersonal skills, emotional understanding, etc. These affected areas often lie at the root of many cases of depression – they certainly have been in my case. If we look at the nature of AS and how it manifests itself, it soon becomes clear that what makes someone Aspergic can also be a major contributor to depression.

Despite often coming across as being cold, logical and emotionless, Aspergic people are still human beings with the need for human contact and social interaction. The general reaction to AS, by the general populace, is to withdraw, either because of ignorance, response to incorrect body-language (as well as the other non-verbal forms of communication), or the inability of the Aspergic person to communicate/behave within accepted/expected limits. This, all too easily, can lead to isolation and a feeling of being excluded. From experience I would suggest that it goes further than this and the difficulties in understanding situations, picking up the subconscious forms of communication, etc., only heighten the feeling of social exclusion – for example you don't 'get' the joke, you miss the implied meaning of something (so you're no longer part of 'the gang').

You now have a person who is, generally, very aware of their environment and other people's seeming reluctance to accept and socialise with them. The problem is, though, what are they supposed to do about it? A non-Aspergic, when faced with a situation of being alone may very well go out, make new friends and develop a new social circle. For an Aspergic this isn't possible (or is very difficult). I've often found that my attempts to talk to people (i.e. to meet new people) have turned into near total disasters as, not wanting to 'scare people off' (or 'information overload' them) I keep the fact that I am Aspergic to myself, but the inability to maintain eye contact, the inability to make smalltalk (in other words, the 'classic' Aspergic traits; or, worse still, the attempts to overcompensate for the 'classic' Aspergic traits) all lead to a very clumsy and stilted conversation. Typically people don't know how to respond when confronted by this 'weird' person who is ever so slightly 'different' (but they can't figure out why he/she is 'different').

Without this social circle though, the isolation becomes even more acute which, typically, leads to withdrawing, backing away from people (both metaphorically and physically), etc. It's something of a vicious circle, and one that's not easy to break. Just as it's difficult to explain that you've got a communication problem, how do you meet new people when you have a problem with smalltalk and are wary of strangers?

Frustrated by frustration

So Aspergic people can often feel isolated and are ill-equipped to get themselves out of this situation, but other factors can also contribute to conditions such as depression. A lot of my depression has stemmed from my work (Is now a good time to plug my article on AS and employment? No? Okay, I won't mention it) and other people's inability to understand or express themselves in terms that make sense to me. The frustration that this causes builds up and, just as with the social vicious circle, feeds on itself.

Everybody, Aspergic and non-Aspergic alike, gets frustrated from time to time (for whatever reason), but releasing that frustration is very important. There are many ways to do this, but the most obvious 'routes' aren't always open to an Aspergic person. Maybe your boss is hassling you, maybe a colleague is annoying you. The solution? Go talk to them. Well that's great if you have that option, but this isn't always a solution that's available to Aspergics. I know that I find approaching even people that I know isn't always easy, and this becomes especially hard when you're going to complain to them about something that they've done or a situation that they've caused. I can think of an event that happened to me recently with my own family, who put me in a very awkward situation (I'm not mentioning details but trust me on this one, I was a mess) and I wasn't able to cope. But it's very difficult to turn round then (to people who are trying to help you) and criticise them for what they've done. Maybe that's just me but I'm acutely aware of upsetting people (it's a gift that I have – being able to upset people that is, not being acutely aware of it) and I tend simply to 'put up' with things rather than express what I'm really thinking and feeling.

Why am I rambling on about all of this? Because it's also a means to explain how Aspergics are ill-equipped to deal with situations and also have an inability to release emotion effectively. The human brain, logical (i.e. Aspergic) or not, is not a machine, it's not a computer and it has 'pointless' aspects to it. Aspects that, seemingly, make no sense but affect our happiness, lives and emotional well-being (even in those of us who are seemingly lacking in certain emotions). The brain, the psyche (call it what you will) has limits and boundaries beyond which it can't cope. The pressures, worries, anxieties that build up within it have to be released, otherwise, in computer terms, it crashes and needs a reboot (and, if you're a real geek, it gets a mental Blue Screen of Death).

Most people have some form of emotional release, but Aspergics aren't always as well equipped. The pressures, anxieties and worries build but can't go anywhere so the depression/paranoia/whatever beast feeds on itself, growing bigger and stronger until something has to snap. This is not to say that depression is solely down to the lack of emotional release, as plenty of non-Aspergics fall into depressive states. Hey, I'm not a psychologist, I'm just someone who's seen a couple of episodes of *Casualty* (a long time ago I'd like to point out – certainly couldn't sit through an hour of that rubbish these days) and knows the thoughts, emotions and feelings that have gone through my Aspergic little head over the years.

Slaying the beast

Mental health problems aren't a given. It's not the rule that simply because you are Aspergic means that you will suffer from some form of mental health problem. As detailed above, I can see *why* there may be additional contributory factors that can lead to states such as depression within Aspergics, but that doesn't mean that all Aspergics should be beating a path to their local lunatic asylum or mental health unit.

So how can depression (sorry, I keep focusing on depression but it's something that I know so I feel confident writing about) be beaten, avoided or treated? The answer is very personal and each individual will beat it in their own way. One thing that is guaranteed *not* to work is to simply 'pull yourself together' as anyone who's never had dealings with depression will advise you to do ('You know what, I never thought of pulling myself together. Hang on while I just give that a try… yep, all better now'). This seems to be the classic response to depression and many 'minor' mental health problems (note: I'm not considering depression to be any less serious than other mental health problems such as schizophrenia, I'm just noting the common perception of it being a 'less serious' form of mental health – hell, at the start of this article I stated that most people don't even think of it as a mental health problem at all).

Realising that you have a problem is the biggest step but, as I know from experience, as you slowly sink into your own little pit of darkness, the light slowly fades and you don't always realise that you're becoming depressed/ill. With a social circle you have people outside looking in, they can see you slipping down into the darkness and, if they're good people, will help. Aspergics, lacking this social circle and also being slightly 'different' to start with, often don't have that 'someone' looking out for them or spotting that they're not coping well (i.e. without knowing someone well, how can you spot when they're changing or going downhill?). Perhaps I'm over-simplifying things or painting a negative picture but I know that this was certainly the case for me during my very lowest of periods – no friends, totally isolated, so no one knew that I was slipping ever downwards... and I certainly couldn't see it from where I was.

An Aspergic on their own can often be seen as very vulnerable to mental health problems. Not only for the fact that no one is looking out for them but also because they have fewer forms of 'emotional release'. I know that even though I was married (past tense) I still became depressed despite having someone there to talk to (which makes writing this really hard as I'm now on my own again and don't have anyone there to act as my 'release valve' – gee thanks, this paragraph really has taken me to places that I didn't want to go to – and that's not a joke, I really am 'churning' inside at having to go through this and 'replay' events from the past).

Being able to talk to people (or even just one person) is very important, but being able to fully release emotions and thoughts is equally important. For the Aspergic this isn't easy, as often you're having to explain and express thoughts, feelings and emotions that you don't understand. And how can you explain to someone else something that *you* have no comprehension of? It's like asking a child to explain quantum physics or string theory with relation to time travel within the Einsteinian universe. (And I did deliberately pick those examples to invoke 'huh?' responses – and, if anyone is interested, actual time travel in the Einsteinian universe isn't possible using conventional three-dimensional movement in space – it's like getting a ball bearing on a table to move 'up'. Hence the need for alternative approaches such as string theory, wormholes and the like. Next week on Theoretical Physics for Beginners, how to demonstrate Heisenberg's uncertainty principle using three paper cups and an old copy of *Caravanning Weekly*.)

My GP once asked me, when I'd gone in with depression following my Aspergic diagnosis (I wasn't depressed about being Aspergic by the way, I was depressed that all of my problems at work hadn't magically been solved by being diagnosed Aspergic) when I'd last been really happy. I couldn't tell him. It wasn't that I didn't know when I'd last been happy, but that I couldn't understand what 'happiness' actually was. (All I understand, in terms of 'happiness', is 'not sad' – defining 'happiness' is, as I understand it, not easy even for non-Aspergics as it's something that you 'feel'. We're back around to the old conundrum: How do I do/explain 'A' when I can't do/ explain 'A'?) These 'gaps' in emotional understanding obviously lead to frustration, the bottling up of emotion, the inability to express yourself fully, and the almost inevitable breakdown if support doesn't exist in the form of someone who understands and can help to fill in those 'gaps'.

Beating depression (and many mental health conditions) relies heavily on identifying the contributory factors – finding out what's at the root of the problem… and, hopefully, fixing it/them. This can sometimes be obvious: death (of someone else that is, if you die then mental health problems, generally, don't really present much of a problem), work (or maybe the lack of), relationship problems, etc. Sometimes the reasons can be more to do with environment – for example house move, the weather (seasonal affective disorder), neighbour trouble. Often though the 'problem' can be a combination of factors, maybe something 'small' that's grown out of all proportion (thanks to the depression/paranoia beast feeding on itself). Whatever the reason, identifying it is crucial not only to get you back on the road to recovery but also to try to avoid the problem from happening again in the future.

Getting help

Identifying that you have a mental health problem isn't always easy (as highlighted above) and figuring out what the causes and reasons behind it can take time. Getting help though is vital. It's not a sign of failure, an admission of weakness or anything to be ashamed of. Being able to put your hand in the air and say 'I have a problem' isn't easy for anyone, but for Aspergics, without that 'encouragement' (either from a social circle, partner, family, etc.) and the added bonus of having to face explaining concepts that are 'alien' it can be a daunting process.

I don't want to go into the specifics of beating depression and mental health problems (there are far better books and articles out there in the big wide world) but as an Aspergic I feel that this is an ideal point to try to encourage and help other Aspergics who might be going through similar problems, and to reinforce the greater need for understanding when dealing with Aspergics, especially when/if the subject of mental health raises its ugly head.

As I've said earlier in this ramble-athon, I am Aspergic, I have been to the depths of depression (and I mean the *very* depths, as in almost taking the 'ultimate solution') and I have managed to survive, sometimes with help, sometimes without. I won't lie and say that it's easy, as it isn't, but mental health problems can be beaten and you can do it – millions of people, including Aspergics, have been there before and come back from the brink.

So what's the secret of surviving mental health problems? For Aspergics it can, from a certain perspective, actually be easier than for NTs. We already live by routine, so establishing a routine and sticking to it is easier for us than it is for 'norms'. Maybe it's just me but I've always retreated back inside myself when I've been hit by depression, I shut the world out and focus on getting through one day at a time. My problems usually stem from work and the lack of friendship so, instead of focusing on work and meeting people, I focus on how to get through the working day and get back to my corner of security. Once you can get through one day then you can get through another. This in itself isn't enough though, as what are you ultimately aiming for? What's the point in getting through the day? This is where establishing goals is vital. Now I'm not talking about aiming to climb Everest, be the first person on Venus or anything, but realistic goals that can be achieved quickly (trust me, if you can see results, even little ones, then it can give you a boost – think about tackling the 'biggies' when you're feeling a bit better). Maybe it's as simple as 'today I'm going to go and buy a newspaper' but it's something that you can do so it's a small step in the right direction.

Setting goals beyond your Aspergic limits is a bad way to start off though. I know that I have a problem making conversation so, instead of jumping in and trying to conquer that particular demon (and being almost guaranteed to fail and then feeling even more worthless) I put it in a box (mentally) and move on to something that I know I *can* do. You might ask why should you do something that you know you can do already, but it's a way to bolster your confidence and shine a little light in your pit of unhappiness. The next thing you achieve makes the light glow a little bit brighter, and so on. I can then revisit the 'difficult' tasks and, if it doesn't go well, the light dims a bit... but it doesn't go out.

Don't let the baskets grind you down

Are you prepared to let the world beat you? I know that I'm not. Yes, I may have a brain that's not wired up properly, most people don't understand me, and the chances of me being elected *Time* magazine's man-of-the-year are slim to none, but I'm not going to let God, nature, work, ignorant <insert rude word here> or anything beat me. I will have bad days, I will get low and I will have to, metaphorically, crawl across broken glass to get where I need to be at times but I, like all Aspergics, am amazing. I exist, I'm here for a reason (from what I can gather this seems to be to make people feel uncomfortable when I'm around, but so be it) and, as Earl Hickey says, 'do good things and good things will happen – do bad things and bad things will happen'. As a piece of logic it sucks it and you can pick holes in it all day long, but trying to live life positively rather than negatively is, I feel, a pretty good starting point.

Chapter 9

A Fairytale Life It Isn't (aka Chapter Nine): Alcohol, Self-harm, and the Benefits of Exercise

Alex Brown

Introduction by Luke Beardon
Alex is one of the most expressive writers I have ever had the privilege of reading; her eloquence is astonishing, and her ability to put into words her feelings and mental states is overwhelmingly exceptional. That Alex has suffered throughout her life (similar to many others in this book) is deeply saddening.

Alex highlights many areas that other people with AS might have issues with. The isolation, the bullying, the knowing that she is different but not knowing why; the terrible feelings of despair and not knowing what to do about it; the constant worry about life in general. And, I suspect, she is similar to many others in that she receives very little support and yet has managed to exist in a world that makes no compensations for who she is and what her needs might be.

One of the first memories I have is when I used to look at myself in the mirror. I used to wonder what I might look like, but mostly I used to wonder what I would be like inside, or how I would feel when I was older. I couldn't recognise the person in the mirror as being me. Someone was staring back at me, but they didn't seem to be connected to me. There is however, a part of me that I can recognise, and that is my eyes. If I look at myself in the mirror, I feel the same as I did when I was three or four looking into the mirror then; that my eyes see what is happening around me, but they also see my thoughts. It is like there being a second pair of eyes that see inwards, and I sometimes feel that I am only a pair of eyes, attached to my brain by ophthalmic nerves, suspended in mid-air. Obviously I am aware of my body to a certain extent, especially when I am running, but it often feels like it isn't a part of me, or it isn't really there, at least in terms of a visual image. I thought that when I grew up I wouldn't feel so sad. I thought I would have control over how I felt, and that the negativity would go away. I thought that when I was an adult all the feelings of insecurity and being unhappy would no longer be there. I used to look at myself and think that maybe it was all a bad dream; it made me feel better to think that one day it would be over and I would be different to the way I was. I think that for some time this was a major disappointment; that when you become an adult you don't change or become a different person, and it is coming to terms with this that is so difficult. Now I can't think of life as just being a bad dream, because I know it is real, and it won't suddenly change or disappear, or worst of all, the same horrible feelings remain.

I can remember, from about the age of four, thinking a great deal about dying. I used to wonder what it would be like; and I imagined it as being asleep, but without dreaming, and never waking up. I found it quite a comforting and peaceful thought.

I had a very protected and happy childhood in respect of my home life. I spent a great deal of time with my family, and my dad in particular always made time for me, and spent most of his spare time with me. I know that I was an extremely anxious child. I had a lot of tantrums as a toddler, but as I grew older, I was eager to please, even though I felt very shy and nervous most of the time. I didn't like being told off, or conflict of any kind. My mum just thought that I was very sensitive, and so when the time came to move to secondary school, they sent me to a small private school because they didn't think I could cope at the local comprehensive.

I never enjoyed school. I'm not entirely sure why, but while I was there I felt in a constant state of anxiety. I started to find life especially difficult once I moved to secondary school. I think I became more aware of the differences between myself and the other pupils. On the one hand I rather liked the fact that I wasn't the same as everyone else, but I also wanted to be able to fit in, or at least I wanted people to like me and to make me feel included. The one girl who was my friend, who wasn't actually very kind to me, moved away. I found it difficult having to change rooms for lessons, and the style of the lessons was different too. I worried a great deal about not understanding the work, and about the fact that I felt so lonely, and why people weren't friends with me. Between the ages of 12 and 16, my mind was pre-occupied with thinking about committing suicide. I think that it was only the dancing, which I did every day during and after school, and my hobby, speedway, which kept me sane.

I started to become paranoid thinking that people were talking about me, and that everyone hated me. I spent my evenings and weekends hiding under my desk in the sitting room that my parents had made for me upstairs. Sometimes I would climb into the wardrobe or airing cupboard and hide in there, to block everything out. I became convinced that the people on the posters on my wall were my only friends, and I would talk to them and tell them how I was feeling. I often felt angry or upset, and I would tell them all sorts of negative things about myself and how bad I was. Then they would tell me bad things about myself too. Sometimes I felt that they could see me, and they were watching me all the time, so I would have to hide under my desk to get away from them. I still sometimes feel like people are watching me if I have a recent photograph of someone. It's like they can see all I do.

I also found that on occasions I was one of the pupils singled out by the teachers at school, presumably because I hadn't understood properly what was being asked of me. They would draw attention to my mistakes in front of the other pupils, and it made me feel humiliated and useless. On one occasion, my French teacher asked me to stand up in front of the rest of the class, and recite the verb *rougir* – to redden. I was perfectly capable of doing this, but I predictably went red, as I always did when I had to do anything in front of other people; and the teacher pointed this out, and said that was the reason why she had chosen that particular verb for me to recite. I don't know if it was her idea of a joke, but I thought it was a cruel thing to do. I remember feeling very unhappy and very angry with everyone and everything at this time. Sometimes when I felt really angry and frustrated I would bang my head against the wall or the door, and hit myself on the head. Or when I was feeling really sad, I would cut my arms with my school compass or a knife. For some reason though, I never felt like I could tell anyone how I was feeling, I guess I couldn't understand why I felt the way I did, and I didn't want to upset my family.

I started drinking in the evenings after school. I stopped eating with my family and was allowed to eat in a separate room on my own. After dinner, I would mix myself a drink from whatever I could find in the house. It didn't make me feel happy, but it took the edge off the anger and sadness that I was feeling. The rest of the time I shut myself away listening to music. One time my cousin came over and popped his head round the door. He asked me how I could listen to such depressing music, but the kind of music I listen to is more a reflection of my mood, than a contributory factor.

I was very keen to go to university. I was desperate to move away from a place that held so many unhappy memories, and I felt like I needed to live independently from my parents. At that time, I think I partly blamed them for the way I felt. I thought that it was their choice of school that had had such a profound effect on my life, although, in reality, it was probably the best thing they could have done. Whilst I did meet some people in my halls of residence, I never formed any friendships as such until the end of my first year at university. This again caused me to feel depressed, and I started to cut myself again, and retreated into the wardrobe in my room. I also felt extremely paranoid, and between lectures I was unable to walk through the cafeteria to join up with other students on my course, or to buy a drink, because I felt like everyone was watching me, and thinking bad things about me. I experienced panic attacks, as I had done when I lived at home, but I was absolutely adamant that I would never go back to living with my parents, or tell them how I was feeling, because I didn't want to feel a failure.

Throughout my teenage years, and into my early twenties, I used to have bouts of depression that would last for months at a time. Sometimes there was a reason, but other times I seemed to feel sad for no discernable reason at all. In the end, my partner felt like he could no longer cope with my moods and the effect that I was having on our relationship, and how I behaved towards him and our daughter. So, basically he told me that I should go to see our GP, because if I didn't try and sort something out, he couldn't see how the relationship would last. I was referred to the community psychiatric nurse, and I met with her on about three occasions. I wasn't sure what I was supposed to be talking to her about. The first couple of times she came to our house, but my partner did most of the talking for me, so she then arranged an appointment at the Health Centre in town. I felt pretty uncomfortable going to see her there, and as I didn't have much to say, she felt that there wasn't much point in us meeting again. Her verdict seemed to be that I had too much time on my hands to dwell on my problems, and that maybe I should consider doing some voluntary work. I guess that occupying my mind may have helped, but I felt dissatisfied at the outcome. I was never made aware of the purpose of the sessions and what I was supposed to do. My GP also gave me some tablets, which he said were for PMT. I took them for a while, but stopped taking them when they showed no sign of improving my mood. In fact I seemed to feel worse, and for much of the time I didn't feel in control at all. I think during this time my behaviour was pretty terrible and unpredictable, and practically unbearable to live with.

I didn't see that I was being irrational, and how I was overreacting to certain situations. I'm not quite sure what my in-laws thought of me at that time. My partner would drive over to their house, and sometimes I'd refuse to go in and see them, and if my partner came out to the car, I'd end up shouting and screaming at him to leave me alone, and would attack him if he came anywhere near me. I felt like I couldn't cope with having anything to do with anyone, including my partner and young daughter. On one occasion when I was feeling stressed out after coming back from a music festival, I said something which resulted in a terrible argument, and I ended up running away. When my partner came looking for me, he found me in a field, hitting myself on the head with a rock. I still feel incredibly guilty about this, because, even though she was only two or three at the time, my daughter remembers the incident vividly.

I suppose I am glad that I haven't committed suicide really. At least at the moment, but I know that when I am feeling really down, I sometimes wish that I had done so at an earlier point in my life. Then I wouldn't have to be going through all this, or my family would have got over it by now, or my partner may have met someone else and been happier with them. I suppose what it really comes down to is I know that I will probably never commit suicide now; and that makes me feel angry with myself when I am feeling bad, but at the same time, it makes me hate myself for considering taking an action which would indirectly or unintentionally hurt my partner and my daughter.

Sometimes I wonder what is going on inside my head. There seems to be something there that I have no control over. I wonder whether it is a part of me, or whether it is something that has entered my head uninvited. There's something unpredictable that gets into my mind and changes me from feeling happy to feeling sad in an instant. It's like flicking a switch, it's that quick, and then I'm sad without any warning and left wondering what's happening to me. I guess there are certain occurrences that trigger it, but all of a sudden it's upon me, like a mist that has come down and enveloped my mind. Sometimes I feel like there is a monster that gets inside my head and pushes me aside. All the sadness I am feeling seems to get bigger and bigger until it's all I can think about. It feels like it will always be there and I don't know how to make it go away and to stop myself from feeling sad.

Sometimes everything hurts. It is because I feel so sad, and I don't think I will ever be able to feel happy, at least not for more than a short period of time. I'm not really sure if it is a pain; but more an ache or uncomfortable feeling over most of my body. It starts in my stomach and spreads up through my chest and into my head. Everything feels tight, and it is difficult to breathe. I feel like I can't move, and even moving my eyes hurts, and sounds hurt my ears. When I cry it hurts inside my head and my chest and throat, and I feel like I can hardly breathe, and I feel like the feeling will never really go away. It feels almost unbearable, and I know that I don't belong anywhere and that I am alone. On one occasion, when I was alone crying in my bedroom, I looked out the corner of my eye, and I saw lots of little black creatures, like beetles, scurrying around on the floor. When I blinked the tears away, they had gone.

When I am feeling very anxious or paranoid I seem to become hypersensitive to light and sound, and if I am in an enclosed area like a doctor's waiting room, I can feel the walls closing in on me, and people's eyes burning into me. If I am walking up the High Street, or in a shop, and I feel really anxious, I find it comforting to repeat a word or phrase over and over again, or tap out a rhythm, and it enables me to get through the experience. When it gets too much at work, I go and curl up on the back seat of the car during lunchtime. I need to be away from everyone, and their voices in particular.

I know it's all in my head, in my mind, but how come it hurts in other parts of your body? How can your heart feel sad? How can it make your arms and legs and chest ache? Why does it make me want to scream at everyone to leave me alone, and make me so intolerant of everyone? I feel like I want to be carefully lifted up by a giant hand, and placed in a box where it's all soft and comfortable and quiet, where no one else can get in.

Sometimes I wonder whether it is because it's what I am used to, that I can't leave it behind, because I don't know what it's like not to have it there? When I was younger I thought I felt bad because I didn't have friends and I didn't think anyone cared about me, which wasn't true because I know my parents must have done. Now I know though that people care about me, but it hasn't stopped me from feeling sad. Sometimes I feel like I just want to shut myself away somewhere and never come out, and never see or talk to anyone else again.

Sometimes I wish I could be someone else. I don't know how other people manage not to feel bad. I don't know whether they don't have the same feelings of sadness, or whether they can ignore them, or they know a way of dealing with them. Sometimes I can't think about anything else. I know it's not healthy, but I just don't seem to be able to take my mind off it. I don't know why I can't tell my parents how I am really feeling. I guess it's because I'm not sure how they will take it. Maybe they won't believe me, or it might make them feel bad. I don't think they'd know what to say. It would just make us all feel uncomfortable, so it's easier to pretend that nothing's wrong.

I used to have this strange notion that people were supposed to be happy, that I would be happy one day. I have been happy on occasions, but now I don't see it as being something that happens naturally, or it isn't like a permanent state that you can exist in. It's there at the top of the well shaft, and you can sometimes catch a glimpse of it, and get closer to it. If you're very lucky, sometimes you are happy for a while, but the smallest doubt or incident can send you right back down again, and it isn't easy making your way back up to the top. I know I seem to have some difficulty in grasping what is really going on, but if there is only me there and I keep away from other people as much as possible, the only person who can be upset by it all is myself. It's not all bad, because you can live in your own private world, and make it what you will; and no one else knows what's going on, or who you are with, and what you are doing. I used to feel so sad when I was younger that I didn't have friends, and thought about all the things I was missing out on, and why other people didn't like me or want to be friends with me. Now though, I find myself thinking that I was so lucky in a way, because whilst I stayed trapped inside my head I was keeping myself safe and away from other people who would no doubt have upset me. I don't know whether it is simply the fact that I have autism, or whether it has a lot to do with being an only child, and experiences I have had, or it may be a combination of all three; but I do need to spend a considerable amount of time on my own, alone with my thoughts.

In order to get through certain periods in my life when I am feeling so down, I have to isolate myself from everyone. I have to shut myself away in the bedroom and curl up and not move at all. I can't seem to be able to bear the sight, sound or touch of another being, and this even includes my cats.

I have a place that I can go to inside my head. I think it is behind my eyes, and I climb inside and hide from the outside world. I don't always hide, but it's a place I can go to, and I can think about things outside of what's going on. Mostly I find myself analysing situations that have happened, or I imagine scenarios that will probably never happen because of the way I am. I like this place, because no one else can ever get in. Sometimes I choose to go there, and sometimes I am just there. It isn't always a happy place to be, but at least I feel I have some control over what happens there. Sometimes people think I am with them, but I'm not. My physical presence is with them, but my mind is not. I think what is different about this place is that I don't come out of it until I am ready to; I don't seem to be able to, no matter what is going on around me. Mostly I like this place, but sometimes it makes me feel more isolated and different and apart and lonely. In a way, it is a safe place for me to retreat to, but sometimes the thoughts and feelings I have in there scare me and unsettle me. Maybe it is because I am aware of my limitations in the real world, and the fact that I can't stay there indefinitely.

Throughout my life I have been aware that I have dreams, but I rarely remember the content of my dreams. I seem to be left with an overall impression, or rather a feeling. Unfortunately it is usually an unpleasant feeling, and I wake up in a state of anxiety, which often lasts for most of the morning.

Some mornings when you wake up it takes a while to remember who you are, or where you are. Or, sometimes you don't know what day it is. I guess when you're feeling down that those are good days, because the terrible days are the days when you wake up and know exactly who you are, what you're supposed to be doing, and you feel full of dread, or scared and unhappy. I guess I've always had a strong sense of obligation or duty, so, however bad it gets, I do what I know I'm supposed to do. Some people give in and maybe think that they know they might be letting other people down, but they can't face it and so don't. Perhaps they have the right idea.

It seems that when I am lacking in confidence, or start getting stressed out too much, I lose the ability to cope with the simplest of things. For some reason, it makes me want to ignore everything, and the smallest of problems develops into a huge worry in my mind. Then I seem to need to make everything else go wrong. This particularly seems to be the case at work. Work is the main cause of stress in my life at the present time.

Sometimes I reach a point where I can't cope with what's happening any more, and I tend to have a bit of a blow out. I feel stressed out about things that have happened at work, and then other little problems build up, until I feel so unhappy and frustrated that I seem to become uncontrollably angry; and then I can't cope with it any more. Usually I take it out on myself, by hitting myself on the head, and banging my head as hard as I can against the table and the door and the kitchen cupboards. I feel like I don't have any control at all, and because I feel so bad and unhappy I want to make everything as bad as it can be. Half the time I don't seem to be aware of what I am doing. Then afterwards I feel completely dazed and exhausted; and incredibly guilty, because it is always my partner, and sometimes my daughter, that has to witness my outbursts. Sometimes it is difficult to separate being generally angry at life from being angry with the people around you. My partner is left wondering what he has said to cause me to react in such a way. Even something as simple as inviting a friend round to our house causes me to totally overreact, or a change to our plans, or having to do something unexpectedly.

At least when I cut myself I can see why it hurts. I'm not sure why it sometimes makes me feel better. In some ways I feel like I need to hurt myself as a sort of punishment for not being able to control my feelings or the factors which make me feel the way I do, and for my lack of understanding for feeling the way I do. Also, if I hurt myself physically, I can concentrate on feeling that hurt, and not the kind that is inside. This doesn't always work, but I can't seem to find any other way to deal with it.

Sometimes I think things, and then they become real in my head. I manage to convince myself that people think bad things of me, and when this happens it makes me feel really sad. Really it's nothing to do with anyone else, just my head messing me around, making me think that everyone hates me and is out to get me. I used to think that I must be a really strong person, and almost invincible, because I am healthy and, despite feeling depressed and wanting to kill myself, I never did; but sometimes I feel like I am a weak kind of person, because I don't think my mind is healthy, and I can't seem to control feeling sad and my mind seems very mixed up.

I have always enjoyed physical exercise, and a few years ago, I took up running. I even joined a local running club, which improved my running no end, and enabled me to experience running in some really beautiful parts of the countryside. I started entering races and enjoyed trying to better my times. I received lots of encouragement from other club members, and even won a trophy for the most improved female athlete at the club. Unfortunately I became injured, and have not been able to run for nearly 18 months. I am recovering from an operation to my knee and will hopefully be back running in a few months time. What I hadn't realised, is how much running and physical exercise affected my mental health. I don't think my injury could really have come at a much worse time for me. My job had recently changed, and I was having difficulty at work. My 14-year-old daughter had just taken an overdose because she was finding life so tough, especially at school; and we were just starting to realise that it was highly likely that myself, my partner and our daughter were all autistic. I know that in general I tend to be a very fidgety, active sort of person, and am not happy unless I am on the go. As a work colleague pointed out to a new member of staff, when I am running it 'keeps me down'. So not being able to dance, run, swim or cycle has had quite a profound effect on my mental state. I find that my levels of concentration are pretty much non-existent nowadays, and I often feel twitchy and like I am itching inside. Most of the time keeping still feels so uncomfortable and my mind seems to flit from one thing to another. I am very easily distracted and find it difficult to stay on task, which is particularly noticeable in a work environment.

At one point I was doing at least one kind of physical activity a day, and it made me feel so much happier. If I was feeling stressed out or angry, I could go for a run or an energetic bike ride, and I would usually come back feeling calmer, having directed my anger and frustration into physical exercise. I guess another aspect about physical exercise is the endorphin hit that it gives you. I love the feeling of utter tiredness, the total physical and mental well-being that it provides. Another aspect I like, is that when you are out on your own, it gives you time to think, knowing that there will be no interruptions from anyone else. You can drift off with your own thoughts, and suddenly you realise that you've covered a couple of miles without even noticing it. Alternatively, you can appreciate the beautiful surroundings if you are lucky enough to live in the countryside.

One place where I usually feel at peace, is in the woodland near my home. I like any woods really, but this one is special to me, probably because I know it so well. It's a place to escape to from the rest of the world, and a quiet place in which to reflect and observe. I like to visit every week if I can, and every time I go there is something different to see, or subtle changes that have taken place. As far as I am aware, I have always been fond of trees. My mum used to take me for a walk in the woods every week before I started school, and I used to like collecting sticks – in fact I still do. It's so relaxing lying down looking up through the branches of the trees and, mesmerised, watching the way the light shines on the leaves. Then there is the sound of the river and the birds, and it feels so good to be away from other people and their voices. It can also be a lot of fun, exploring hidden parts of the wood, climbing trees and making dens hidden out of sight. We tend to spend quite a lot of time together there as a family, and I think we have made a lot of discoveries about ourselves because it feels easier to discuss things in such a beautiful and peaceful environment.

I was thinking that it isn't being different that is a problem, and I don't want to be like an NT person particularly, but really I just want to be accepted by people sometimes or not be made to feel that I am so odd or a horrible person. I suppose that really it is down to other people to alter their perception of what makes a good person, or at least to accept people's differences without making them feel they are in some way a freak.

I suppose it's the experiences I have had throughout my life that have led me to have such low self-esteem. I know that I am extremely sensitive to any form of criticism – it's not that I believe I am right, or what I am doing is perfect; but more the fear of failure and humiliation, and the fact that I feel that so many parts of my life have been unsuccessful. If I were to consider this on another day, I might feel that I have made a success of certain things. For instance, my partner and I have been together for 18 years and have a daughter we are both really proud of. There have been lots of sad and difficult times – mainly based around work and other people; but there have also been lots of happy and fun times too. I guess life may have been easier in some respects, if we had known that we had autism at an earlier stage in our lives, rather than in our mid to late thirties, but at least now we can understand why we feel the way we do, and try to avoid some of the situations which cause us unhappiness and conflict.

Chapter 10

'Getting My Life Back': A Mother's Struggle to Get Mental Health Services for Herself and Her Son

Anne Henderson

Introduction by Luke Beardon
As with the other chapters of this book this makes for traumatic reading – but
Anne is absolutely right in that the experiences of the past should be used to
make sure the same mistakes are not made twice. I hope that her contribution
will make a positive change to practice, and that her message gets to be heard
by the right people.

Anne mentions suicide – and is not the only author in this book to do so.
She notes that she believes that when a person with AS mentions suicide it is
likely that the person is very serious – and should be taken very seriously. I
agree that all people who mention suicide should be taken seriously, whether
they have AS or not. Anne also mentions the concept of choice, and the fact
that suicide appeared to be the only choice for her son – this is an extremely
important point to make, as I suspect many people with AS find it difficult to
recognise what their choices might be, particularly at times of stress. The phrase
'there is always a choice' is not applicable for many people with AS much of
the time – perceptually at least. It may well be that appropriate support should
focus on exploring what choices are available to the individual, and enabling

the individual to achieve alternative choices, as opposed to going down a more traditional route of treating the individual as being mentally ill.

My son has Asperger syndrome which was not diagnosed until he was in his late twenties and that was about ten years ago – I have been asked to write of my experiences trying to access mental health services for both my son and myself; what happened cannot be changed but some really simple approaches and common sense could have turned a nightmare into a positive outcome for all concerned. My son knows that I am writing about our experiences and feels as strongly as I do about improving services for people with AS and, in turn, for professionals, carers and everyone in the wider community involved with AS individuals.

As a baby my son was very late talking and my first encounter with a long string of professionals was with a child psychiatrist who stated that he was brain-damaged and would never talk or progress beyond age 2 and a half years – this statement was a damning label and totally unjustified as it has turned out. The damage was horrific; I was totally unprepared for such a bald statement and it has always stayed with me, the shock, the fear and the guilt of thinking that it was something that I had, or had not, done to cause this and, above all, my fear and ignorance of this alien mental health/learning disability world. I had no experience of coping with mental illness or learning disability – other people had these problems not me. Fortunately, things have changed over the years but the stigma of being different in society, particularly if it concerns the mind, and intolerance of eccentric behaviour are still prevalent.

After six months of intensive speech therapy my son had caught up with his speech, but it was very pedantic and he lived life by his own rules – once a routine had been set it was set for ever and the slightest change was enough to instigate extreme anxiety. School was not easy, and again he was labelled disruptive, but he persevered in spite of not fitting in and always being the fall guy for his peers. Again, professionals, educational psychologists, psychologists, psychiatrists, speech therapists, an endless list of people, insisted that he did not have a problem but was just difficult and, as one GP said, 'a bad lot'. At one assessment by a well-known educational psychologist we were told that my son had been 'over educated' – a totally baffling statement! This meant that his education was totally mainstream which had its good and bad points. This situation continued into his time at college, training schemes and working life; he knew that he was different and could not understand why he did not 'fit in' in the conventional sense. The pressure on him must have been intense as he struggled to make sense of a non-AS world with all its social complexities that are taken for granted by people without AS. One aspect that stays with me always is his lack of resentment of the treatment he has received – he is so forgiving and vulnerable to being blamed when a culprit for a misdemeanour is needed in our society.

By this time he was working as a gardener and lodging independently, but the stress was beginning to build up and his behaviour became very bizarre. He was eventually admitted to a secure learning disability ward, the only possible option, but totally inappropriate for him and the other patients, and difficult for staff with no apparent knowledge of or training in AS – it was about the time of his discharge that he was diagnosed with Asperger syndrome by which time our relationship was under severe strain. He was discharged into a hostel for the homeless, a nightmare for him with his need for routine and his inability to cope with change. Eventually after a period of inappropriate housing he moved into his own flat and started an IT course at a college that specialised in supporting students according to their needs. This was a year where he was happy and coping well, but at the end of the year the funding ran out and he tried to find work without success. The disappointment and frustration of not having a purpose to get up each day and having no social life eventually led to him being sectioned under the Mental Health Act as he no longer wanted to live and suicide became a real threat.

I think that the day he was sectioned was the worst day of my life and, if it was like that for me, I cannot imagine what it must have been like for him trying to understand what was happening to him and why. I received a telephone call at midday to say that it was going to happen, but with very little explanation – all in a day's work to an approved social worker, but totally terrifying to patient and carer. I went to visit him the next morning on the ward, again with no explanation of procedures and I was not even sure who were patients or staff. Fortunately admission has become more humane over the past few years and I understand that there is now some literature available to explain the procedure. But the worst was yet to come – two days after admission I was told that there was absolutely nothing wrong and that he should not be in hospital.

I have subsequently talked to people with AS and several world-class AS specialists who have told me that when someone with AS talks about committing suicide it is a very real possibility as, logically, suicide is the only option left.

My son was given very mixed messages, and his eventual transfer to the psychiatric hospital where AS was understood was horrific – real 'One Flew over the Cuckoo's Nest' stuff. The planning for the transfer was virtually non-existent, staff refused to listen to me that he was somehow moving mountains of his possessions from his flat to the ward where he had been given a room on his own as he could not cope with some of the other very ill patients. He had over the years developed OCD and the more unwell he became the more possessions he insisted on having with him. The day came and he had asked me to be there for the move; all went well until it came to loading his belongings – expected by the staff to be a suitcase. Imagine their horror when mountains of possessions, all neatly packed, began to appear from his room – to this day I cannot understand how they did know what was in his room! He would not be parted from his things and they just shouted louder and threatened the police be called to move him – my companion and I asked for a few minutes with him and we managed to calm him enough to load two large cars and get him into a car but the vision of a nurse with a syringe at the ready will always be there.

Fortunately, this move was to a hospital where, as I have said before, AS was understood, and it was the start of a very long three years for him, but with a good outcome and the first step to as he says 'getting my life back'. Gradually the drugs he had been put on were changed and he began to look more like his old self – he began to eat more appropriately and relearn good habits, and the more important stage began where absolutely everyone involved with him gave him consistent messages and he had a very clear plan for his week. There were regular care planning meetings and excellent input from everyone involved in his care. This meant that he knew exactly what was expected from him and he also had a place where he could have his say. From this point he moved to a second placement where he started college again with appropriate support, and he continues to move towards a happier future. He made his last move when the section was lifted ten days short of three years. He is now living in a house with five other people with AS and is learning to budget and access the community successfully, and he has enrolled for the next academic year to continue his studies. There are frustrations and always will be, but at last he has a future to look forward to and an aim to have his own front door and a job and also to be part of the community.

As I have said before we are lucky as a family to have weathered the past 36 years and, whilst I know there is change happening at last, there are a few commonsense, simple changes which can dramatically improve the lot of Aspies who are unfortunate enough to cross paths with mental health authorities and professionals. In my view they are:

- Increase awareness in all sectors of Asperger syndrome and its basic problems and, most importantly, recognise the many strengths of Asperger's not just the negatives.

- Listen to Aspies – there is almost always a reason for challenging behaviour – good planning and support can prevent a crisis and huge expense. Planning for any change is absolutely crucial for anyone with Asperger's to achieve success.

- Appreciate how logical AS thinking is – when behaviour seems eccentric try and work out the steps of thinking used without the frills built in by social convention.

- Acknowledge that carers are a good resource – they know what triggers increased anxiety and can recognise early signs of people becoming unwell, they know the history and are usually the only constant as professionals and care workers come and go with regularity.

- Establish good communication and co-operation between all agencies and patient and carer as being essential to achieve a good outcome for everyone – a basic respect for each other does not cost anything and may even prevent duplication.

These are very much my personal observations of living with someone with Asperger's, but even though at times life has been hard for us I would not change anything; I have learnt so much and I now feel passionate in helping to improve quality of life for anyone involved with AS be it the Asperger individual, family/carer or provider. To work together as a team with realistic expectations must be better than a 'them and us' situation.

Chapter 11

A Week in the Life Of: Strategies for Maintaining Mental Health as an Aspie

Steve Jarvis

Introduction by Luke Beardon

Steve comments on a number of different techniques/therapies that may assist in the reduction of stress and anxiety, and increase esteem and build confidence. He also makes the important point that what works for one person may not work for another. Steve places particular emphasis on physical exercise; he is not alone in believing that physical activity can reduce stress and anxiety. Other authors in this book have commented on exercise as a beneficial activity; however, it should not be assumed that all people with AS can use exercise as an antidote to stress – for some, in certain circumstances, such activity can bring about its own anxieties. Swimming, for example, can be a stressful experience – the sharing of changing rooms and the pool can be a preclusive component in themselves for example, or the sensory environment may not suit. I am not suggesting that exercise should not be seen as an extremely useful strategy – simply that the wider 'society' needs to recognise that adaptations should always be considered in order to benefit those with AS.

Like a lot of people with Asperger syndrome (AS) I have suffered from levels of anxiety and depression that have been detrimental to my mental and physical health, and it's only in the last few years that I have found effective strategies to reduce these debilitating mental health problems. I am 46 years old. I was diagnosed a year ago.

As a child I used to hide behind the sofa whenever a stranger came to the door, and I am told that I was terrified by men in white coats for months after an operation at 18 months of age to correct a squint. The clinical staff had to restrain me for a short time after surgery to stop me from pulling the bandages off my eyes.

When I started my first office job, my heart would skip a beat whenever a phone rang. I experienced high levels of fear and anxiety most days. This would be particularly the case whenever I was not in control of my environment, which would frequently be the case at work and in social situations. I did not know that I had AS, and I think my family and I just thought I was a shy introvert. With both the anxiety and the depression I tended to suffer in silence. I did not feel able to discuss these problems with anyone else. Instead I tried to escape my condition though drink and obsessive watching of films and TV.

In my late twenties I reached a really low point. I had started to write morbid poetry in drunken stupors, and I rarely socialised – isolating myself more and more and deepening the depression. My family would puzzle over why I never opened my curtains in any room of my house. At the age of 28 I visited a Jungian psychotherapist. I picked him out of the Yellow Pages. I was too ashamed to consult my GP first. I paid in advance for 12 sessions. I soon learned that he was more interested in talking to me about his ambition to make lots of money from writing popular horror stories, such as those written by Stephen King and James Herbert, than listening to me. He knew that I had most of their books and asked to borrow them. I think he wanted to learn the 'recipe' for success with such writing. I got more and more dejected as I realised that he did not seem to be that interested in helping me, even after I had made some deeply private disclosures relating to a sexual obsession. Fourteen years later when I reached rock bottom again, I had learned from this unpleasant experience and I did consult with my GP who gave me a list of recommended counsellors. I visited a wonderful man who started me on my current path to a happier way of life, largely free of depression and extreme anxiety. The reason for sharing this personal experience is to stress the importance of seeking professional advice for counselling or psychotherapy services. There are people out there willing to exploit the gullible nature of many people with AS.

A year before I reached rock bottom for the second time, I received a shock when I was diagnosed with alcohol neuropathy. This serious disorder involves decreased nerve functioning caused by damage that results from excessive drinking of alcohol. I gave up alcohol for six months and now I keep a written record of every unit I drink to ensure I keep under the healthy limit for men of 21 units a week. I have mentioned this, because it highlights the risk to health from trying to deal with high levels of anxiety and depression with alcohol.

One of the most effective therapies that I have tried for reducing my anxiety has been neurofeedback or electroencephalogram biofeedback. You may not be familiar with this therapy so I will describe what it involves through my own personal experience. I expect though that the process I describe varies somewhat between therapists. I started with a one-hour consultation that involved my therapist gathering information about my case history with the objective of agreeing realistic goals for the neurofeedback. Examples of some of my goals were:

- reduce my social anxiety and hypervigilance (4)

- increase my confidence, and positive attitude (5)

- increase passion and empathy with others, especially with intimate relations (2).

The therapist asked me to score myself from 1 to 10 on where I thought I was against these goals. These are the numbers in the brackets. The consultation also served the purpose of confirming that neurofeedback was the right therapy for me. I should state at this point that I had not been diagnosed with AS at the time of this therapy. I thought I suffered from alexithymia, which is a condition characterised by difficulties identifying, and describing emotions in self and others. Recent research indicates that alexithymia does overlap with AS.

The next session was the initial assessment, which lasted about four hours. The therapist fixed electrodes at particular positions on my head and measured the strength of the brainwaves between these positions as various frequencies as she asked me to perform simple tasks (e.g. playing games like PacMan, reading a passage, imagining an image). I did not find this assessment too stressful. There was no need to shave my head, though I did need to try to stay relaxed as I focused on the tasks. The therapist discovered that I had low brainwave patterns in many parts of my brain, but particularly at the front.

The next phase is the training. I visited the therapist twice a week for one hour. I kept a diary recording any evidence of change against my goals between sessions. This might be a description of how I felt a particular social interaction went at work or with friends. The therapist decided, based on this evidence and my response to questions at the start of the session, what training to do. Basically this means which positions on my head to place the one or more electrodes. In my case we started by addressing my social anxiety and focused on the front of the right hemisphere of my brain. The training uses the same principles that Pavlov used to get his dog to salivate at the sound of a bell. You get rewarded by a long audio sound, or lengthening a coloured bar on a computer screen when the brain is producing brainwaves above a set threshold in the parts of the brain being trained. I needed to be as relaxed as possible, which I found difficult. I struggled to master abdominal breathing, which was one of the relaxation techniques used. The therapist monitored my performance from her terminal and gave me any verbal feedback that she thought was necessary. I completed 42 sessions and my score for the social anxiety goal changed from 4 to 7.5. This was the largest increase of all my goals. I found that I stopped getting panicky in crowds and I was more relaxed and confident before social interactions with strangers. I did find this therapy challenging and stressful, not helped by the fact that I suffer from perfectionism. I had problems with insomnia and sometimes I lost confidence in my ability to change. I think the therapy was much less useful in addressing my difficulties with emotions and empathy. I think GPs do sometimes refer children for this therapy for conditions such as ADHD. I had to get my treatment privately, and it is expensive.

I have discovered that some research has been done to study whether neurofeedback can reduce anxiety in adolescent boys diagnosed with AS (Scolnick 2005). The findings indicate that this therapy may be beneficial, but as yet there have not been large enough sample sizes to generate conclusive results.

I thought it might be helpful to describe a typical week in terms of what I do to try to manage my anxiety and to maintain confidence and a high self-esteem to mitigate the risk of falling into a depressed state.

It is Monday evening and I have had a particularly stressful day. I am preoccupied about how I will cope with a difficult meeting later in the week and I do not know how to resolve an issue that I have with a colleague. I notice the stress through the tension in my body. I decide to go for an early evening walk in the local park. I find exercise an excellent way of reducing stress levels, although I never exercise late in the evening as this can make it more difficult to sleep. I still feel tension in my body after the walk, so I decide to lie on my bed and play my progressive relaxation and breathing tape. Progressive relaxation involves systematically tensing and then relaxing sets of muscles in the body. I find this one of the most effective methods of getting into a relaxed state.

Every other Tuesday I am a helper at a local social club for adults with learning disabilities. I find this immensely rewarding. I can sometimes feel a little down from negative thinking, but once I am at the club this soon lifts as I am forced out of myself to interact with the club members. I think it can be difficult to find the motivation to start voluntary work if you are very depressed. I needed to address some of the causes of my mental health problems through counselling and other therapies before I felt able to try voluntary work.

It is Wednesday and I am noticing that I am more and more preoccupied by how I will cope with the meeting on Friday. I decide to do what I do for most meetings and write down a plan for how I should approach the meeting. I write down the objectives of the meeting. I write down how I should respond to likely scenarios. This is my way of feeling more in control of an unpredictable situation. I am like most Aspies in that I like to be in control. I get anxious when I am put in a situation that I cannot control. Planning is my tool for managing these situations and I do not think I could do the job I do without it.

It is Thursday evening and the day before my meeting. I feel the need for a boost of confidence. I decide to listen to my *Build Your Self Esteem* CD by Glenn Harrold. There are many similar self-help products that claim to boost self-esteem and confidence. I like this one, because it seems to be very effective at getting me quickly into a very relaxed state and it does not rely on visualisation too much. I have discovered that I am poor at visualising in my mind's eye. I speculate that the early childhood trauma of the eye operation may have affected the development of my visualisation ability, as I can visualise touch and movement, but not sight, sound or smell. I imagine that touch would have been a key sense for me as I lay in bed at 18 months of age restrained and blindfolded after the eye surgery. The last few minutes of this CD involve repeating positive affirmations. I find affirmations a powerful tool to help increase my confidence. I have even made a tape of my favourite affirmations to play in the car on the way to work. Here is one example: 'I am a worthwhile person who is growing in confidence all the time.' An affirmation is a positive statement that is worded in the present tense. Stating that something will happen in the future is not sending your mind the right message (e.g. 'I will be a worthwhile person...').

During the meeting on Friday I notice that the muscles in my neck are tense. I take a few, slow, deep abdominal breaths and then tense and relax my hands and neck. Usually this goes unnoticed by the others in the meeting. Sometimes I find an excuse to leave the meeting briefly to have more privacy to do these powerful relaxation techniques.

It is Saturday morning and I walk to my yoga class. I find yoga a great way to start the weekend, particularly after a stressful working week. It seems to have many positive benefits for me from helping strengthen my weak back to emptying my mind of preoccupations and generally getting me in a relaxed and positive state.

It is Saturday afternoon and I am about to meet a friend for coffee. This is a fairly regular event and I look forward to it. In the past I had great difficulty contacting friends when I felt lonely and in need of some social interaction. The thought going through my mind was often 'They don't want to be bothered by me contacting them'. I now realise that it was that kind of thinking that often pushed me into depression, when the best thing I could have done would have been to pick up the phone and contact the friend. I think it is so important to address the issue of low self-esteem first, because it is this that will help give the confidence to ring that friend when you are feeling the need to talk. I have discovered that talking to a friend is one of the best ways for me to release pent up emotions.

The week ends with my singing group on Sunday evening. I love singing and this seems to help me be more spontaneous and perhaps put me in a state of mind where I am better able to connect to my emotions. I think doing something you enjoy in a group is a wonderful way to keep healthy in every way.

I have recently discovered that sharing experiences with other AS people through discussion forums and social groups is helpful when it comes to mental health issues.

I love books and I collect them on a range of subjects. I recommend Dr Turner's book *Anxiety, Your Questions Answered*, which concisely answers all the common questions a professional, parent or sufferer may have on the subject of anxiety.

I cannot comment on the use of antidepressant drugs, because I have not taken any. I do occasionally take mild sleeping pills when I am anxious about sleeping the night before a challenging meeting at work. I do not think this is to be recommended, but it is my way of surviving a stressful job. I plan to retire early as I am noticing that the years of anxiety and stress are beginning to show in my body. I have fractured teeth from grinding in my sleep. I have varicose veins from a bad habit of crossing my legs tightly when stressed.

Finally, I think it is important to stress that what works for one person may not work for another. I think it is important to try different things and see what works for you. My poor ability at visualisation has meant therapies that use visualisation such as cognitive behavioural therapy (CBT), neuro linguistic programming (NLP), and eye movement desensitisation and reprocessing (EMDR) appear to be less helpful for me. One of these may be the best therapy for you to reduce your mental health problem, such as anxiety.

References

Scolnick, B. (2005) 'Effects of electroencephalogram biofeedback with Asperger's syndrome.' *International Journal of Rehabilitation Research 28*, 159–163.

RECOMMENDED RESOURCES

Harrold, G. (2003) *Build Your Self Esteem* (Audio CD). Diviniti Publishing Ltd.

McKay, M. and Fanning, P. (1991) *Progressive Relaxation and Breathing* (Audio tape). New Harbinger Publications.

Turner, T. (2003) *Anxiety, Your Questions Answered.* Churchill Livingstone.

Chapter 12

My Plastic Bubble: Dealing with Depression, Anxiety, and Low Self-confidence

Wendy Lim

Introduction by Luke Beardon

Wendy writes a personal account that I am sure will resonate with many people with AS. The overriding feeling of fear through childhood, and the recognition of being different but not knowing why, and the stress of not knowing how to behave without being treated negatively – these are all experiences that frequently occur for people with AS. What is so disgraceful is that simple acceptance of difference – indeed an embracing of difference – would surely go a long way to reducing or eliminating such horrendous experiences. Of course, in reality, the paradigm shift in neurotypical thinking towards acceptance of people with AS – and all the natural ways of AS behaviour – is far from simple. AS is not something that is easy for NTs to understand, and it is easy to understand why there is no easy way to bring about such a dramatic change in understanding of AS and, thus, acceptance. However, just because it is not a simple process does not necessarily make it the wrong one, and Wendy's account of her own experience should give everyone a sharp reminder of how much of an impact the environment (mostly people) can have on people with AS.

From the time that I went into the very social world of school I felt that not only was I very different to my peers, but that I was inherently defective in some way. Since early childhood I have never fitted in anywhere and have always had a strong feeling that I am not normal. I always sensed that there was something wrong with me that set me apart from the rest of the human race. That something seemed to repel people and make me a figure of fun; *something* rather than *someone*, there to be ridiculed. I suspected that everybody except me knew what that something was and that nobody could tell me because they thought it would be too hurtful or too shameful for me to hear, and possibly too embarrassing for them to say. And so the whole world was keeping it a secret from me and could only talk about it, and about me, in hushed tones behind my back. In a way I was right; I was different and there were some things, such as my lack of eye contact and 'odd' gestures and body language which a person would need to be on the outside of me in order to observe, and that I wouldn't have been aware of unless someone had pointed it out to me. But in a way I couldn't have been more mistaken. The problem was that when I was growing up in the 1960s and 70s, nobody did know what was 'wrong' with me. After having spent over a decade seeing more counsellors and mental health professionals than I can count (not one single one of them picked up on what the was the root cause of my difficulties), and after looking in various self-help books and psychology books for answers as to why I am the way that I am, I was finally diagnosed with Asperger syndrome at the age of 42.

For so many years I thought I was mentally ill and that I must have somehow got incredibly messed up psychologically, although I couldn't quite see how. And then in my early forties I found myself needing to come to terms with a new identity as a person who has a condition that is, for me, disabling and that isn't going to go away; meaning that I am always going to be pretty much like this. This meant that I needed to let go of certain dreams and ambitions that I had. For instance, I had thought that if I ever 'got better enough' I would like to be a counsellor or some kind of support worker. I now know that can't ever happen. Instead I hope to be able to reach people through my writing.

Looking back to when I was a young child, the only emotion I can remember feeling was fear. I was frightened of any machine that made a noise, and I used to be wary of anything which was brought into the home that I wasn't familiar with and that I wasn't used to having around. Being taken on the London Underground, and particularly the deep level lines, was one of the most terrifying experiences that I could be subjected to. The noise that the train made when it came into the station was so unbearably loud that being taken down there felt like a threat to my life. It was excruciating noise overload for me; more than my brain could take at that time. Although I still have some sensory issues around using the tube, I now find it really interesting and sometimes I travel around on it just for fun. In other ways though, not much seems to have changed since I was a little girl. Back then I was frightened of so many people and things, it begged the question 'Was there anything I wasn't scared of?' I didn't realize that it wasn't like that for all children. In many ways I am still very much that frightened little girl. Not much has changed since I was about six years old or younger in terms of my relationship with fear and the way that I deal with fear. The difference is that I now have an 'inner mother' who can think rationally and who can take care of that child, so I don't need to feel quite so powerless in the face of my fear. As a child I found people terrifying; some more so than others. I used to be frightened of some people because of the way they looked, even though they were always kind to me and never did anything to make me fear them. Some people I was scared of simply because they paid attention to me. I still find people frightening. It has taken me all my life to learn how to live in the neurotypical world and how to adapt, and I am still learning. To me, everybody is an alien. Some of them are friendly aliens and some of them are not so nice, but they are all aliens and everyone is potentially the enemy. I have often felt that I haven't got a clue how to speak to another human being.

I imagined that when I reached a certain age I would start to feel 'grown up', but that time has never come. Although I now have adult children, I have never really felt adult enough to be a parent. I wouldn't know what it is like to feel like an adult because I never have. I have never stopped feeling like a child; not a happy, carefree child who can run around and climb, and swing upside down, and shout, and laugh, and cry, and play, and fight, and come home filthy. I never was that child. The child I have remained is a child who is terrified of her own shadow. Some things, such as learning to drive a car, I have never even seriously thought about doing, I have never felt adult enough to. I still feel like a little girl who always expects other people to be angry with me and to berate me if I do the slightest thing wrong or not to their liking. This makes it very difficult for me to assert myself with my adult children. I have often felt that they are trying to take control of our home environment, and in these situations I tend to be like a mute child and become very incoherent when I try to make my feelings known and take some control of my living space. Although the situation seems to have improved recently and I am hopeful that things will continue to gradually get better, in relation to my adult sons I tend to feel like a child who has very little choice, not much say and not much control over how the home environment is. I know that it is not satisfactory and it is not normal for a parent to feel so out of control, and these feelings cause me very high levels of anxiety. I realize on some level that I probably do have a lot more power and more control than I think I have, but it is because I feel like a powerless child that home doesn't always feel like a safe place for me to be. My idea of heaven would be to feel in control of my life and not to feel frightened all the time. Wherever I go and whatever I do, even when I am doing something that I find pleasurable, it is hard for me really to enjoy anything to the full because there is always an undercurrent of anxiety there. And yet I feel that to some extent my anxiety protects me because it may keep me alert to the possible dangers around me, although I guess that my fear is out of proportion to any realistic threat posed to me. At its worst it can mean that at times I am living almost in a state of fight or flight. The problem with anxiety is that if it is long-term, as mine has been, we can become so conditioned to feeling that way that it becomes normality for us. Those feelings of dread can remain long after the original cause of the anxiety has passed.

When my anxiety levels are at their highest, it is sometimes because I have withdrawn into my own world and neglected to do things that I really should have done. When I realize that time is running out for me to do those things, or when the consequences of my not having done them start to catch up with me, that is when panic sets in and my anxiety spirals out of control. When this happens, the only thing for me to do is to give myself a big push to tackle those things that need to be done. That is the only way that I am going to reduce my anxiety. For most of my life I have lived in a very messy environment, often in squalor, surrounded by clutter. This is partly because I am a hoarder and hate to let go of anything, and it is mainly because I have so little interest in housework. I have always found it very difficult to get motivated and to organize myself to do household chores. I am a bit clumsy and uncoordinated anyway, and because I was inexperienced at doing household chores they seemed massive. It was hard for me to sequence the small tasks involved in getting the whole job done. There seemed to be so many steps to pass through in order to complete the whole task that it seemed to take forever. I developed a kind of housework phobia and stopped trying to do even the most basic chores around the house. Things got on top of me to point where I felt that so much clutter had accumulated that it could never be cleared, and the dirt seemed so ingrained that it couldn't be cleaned away. I gave up the fight. I paid a high price for this because I lived in constant fear of the consequences of not doing any housework. I dreaded visitors coming because then they would see how we were living. It also caused a lot of conflict with my husband who used to try to clean up. My autism outreach worker spent a lot of time cleaning with me and helping me to clear some of the clutter. This turned out to be just what I needed; somebody finally understood that I wasn't just lazy; it wasn't that I couldn't be bothered and it hadn't been my choice to live in squalor. I never used to think of myself as a 'morning person', but I have found that the only time of day when I can switch to a kind of 'cleaning mode' when I don't too much mind doing some cleaning and some tidying up is in the very early hours of the morning when the rest of the world is still asleep. I have trained myself to get up very early for this purpose and I have come to associate this time of day with cleaning, so I know that I will get *some* work done. I know that the session isn't going to go on forever, because at a certain time I stop and for the rest of the day I do what *I* want to do. I also know that I am not going to get any work done at any other time of day and that I would greatly resent doing it at any other time.

In my experience, one of the greatest barriers to good mental health is poor self-esteem. It can also be one of the greatest barriers to being able to have healthy and mutually satisfying relationships with other people.

Ever since I can remember I have felt like some kind of freak. Before I knew about Asperger syndrome I knew that I didn't particularly like being the way that I am but felt very limited in my power to change. Knowing that I was different to other people but not knowing why has done serious and possibly irreparable damage to my self-esteem. I see self-confidence and self-esteem as being two very different things. Self-confidence is about knowing where my strengths and weaknesses lie, and having faith in my ability to do things. I may not, for instance want to clean the kitchen floor; there might be dozens of other things that I would rather do. But whilst I may not enjoy doing it, I know that I *can* do it. I have done it countless times before, so I know that I can do it again, i.e. I have confidence in my own ability to do the task. Self-esteem, on the other hand, relates to my self-image, how I perceive myself as a person and how I imagine that others see me. Nobody, whether disabled or otherwise, comes into the world with poor self-esteem. The damage is often done by other people through their attitudes and their reactions towards us. Although I learned to talk early, so I am told, throughout my life I have suffered from what is known as 'selective muteness' which becomes worse in situations where I feel under most pressure to speak or when I feel overwhelmed by the social demands being placed upon me. As a child I was often in trouble because I didn't answer when I was spoken to. And the more I go out into the community, the more I get asked 'Why are you so quiet?' 'Why don't you speak?' 'You never talk to anyone, why not?' Or people make comments behind my back which I may overhear, or I might be told about them later. The more I put myself out there, and if I do speak, that is when it becomes apparent how 'odd', how socially unskilled and how out of touch with ordinary people I really am. All the time that I stay quiet, people will think I am just that: quiet. They will think I am weird for that too though! That has been my identity since early childhood: shy, quiet, doesn't speak. And people find that baffling. They don't understand why, and people have often let me know in no uncertain terms that they think I am strange. I guess that they just don't know what to make of me. I have even been asked if I can speak by people who were,

I think, rude and ignorant and they just reinforced my feelings of shame. They enhanced the feeling I already had that it is not alright for me to be the way that I am; as though I have a disease that I *should* want to be cured of at any cost and that I *should* be bending over backwards to change. I was bullied throughout school because of the difficulty that I have integrating myself socially. They didn't seem to understand that it wasn't my choice to be this way and that it wasn't just a case of me being a snob and not trying to be sociable. Also, due to gross motor dyspraxia, I was just about the worst in the school at any kind of sports. As an adult this doesn't matter, but at school a lot of playground games involve running and playing with balls; two of the things that I found extremely difficult. So even when I was included in playground games, it was an ordeal for me. This gave the other children something else that they could ridicule me over because they said I 'ran funny' and they used to mimic the way that I ran. I couldn't throw or catch a ball either, and PE lessons were something that I dreaded. I mention this here because it was one more thing that made me stand out as different to my peers and made me feel that I was just not normal in any way. It was something else that I felt painfully self-conscious about.

Even after I had children of my own I still used to get made fun of, and on occasions my property has been vandalized by children and youths who saw me as a 'nutter' and as somebody who is vulnerable and easily scared, i.e. somebody who merits no respect and who it is fun to pick on. I have often been called weird, crazy, mad, and that became my identity; especially when I was younger and before I knew about Asperger syndrome. I came to see myself in that way too, because I thought so many people couldn't all be wrong. I could see that they did have a point because I do stand out as different and as strange. That negative self-image has been with me for a lifetime and it has become so deeply ingrained within me that it isn't going to go away just because I get a diagnosis. I don't know if it can ever go away.

Seeing my own reflection in the mirror when I am at home in the privacy of my bedroom or bathroom isn't a problem for me. But I hate catching sight of my reflection when I am out in public, and I will avoid sitting near a mirror where I can see my reflection. This is because I am then seeing myself as the outside world sees me and I seem to look quite different then. I will not have my voice recorded in any way or under any circumstances, because I might hear that recording being played back at some time and I really don't think I could survive the embarrassment, the shame and the emotional pain of hearing myself as other people hear me. That would honestly feel like a threat to my continued existence. I know that I sound odd when I speak, especially when I am under pressure to talk. It was pointed out in my diagnostic report that my speech is what they called monotone; I have also been told that I talk rather slowly. Sometimes I sound like a rather sad and serious little, little girl. Sometimes I think I sound like a robot or like an alien; not human, like something not of this world. Not infrequently I have the same kind of difficulty stringing a sentence together that somebody who has English as a second language might have. It is something that I feel very self-conscious about. And those feelings of embarrassment and self-consciousness cause me more stress, which makes the problem worse. If I could find a way of feeling more comfortable around people, my social skills might improve of their own accord. Writing or typing is a much easier way for me to communicate and to express myself. I am also looking into the possibility of learning sign language.

I don't particularly wonder what I would be like if I didn't have Asperger syndrome. But I do wonder what I would be like with just AS, but without being further disabled by depression, anxiety, especially social anxiety, low self-confidence and serious self-image problems. I am an introvert by nature, a quiet, shy person, and I daresay I would have been even without AS. It is hard for me to know how many of my difficulties are due to Asperger syndrome and how much I am disabled by extreme shyness and severe social anxiety, which I think might be half my problem. The fact that I don't usually say much and I tend not to speak unless I am spoken to may have been my saving grace at times though. It may have saved me, on occasions, from seriously embarrassing myself, from 'putting my foot in it' and causing serious offence to others.

I have mixed feelings about having Asperger syndrome. I can now put into words that on some level I am angry that I have AS and, yes, I am angry with myself for having it. Even though that anger is, I know, pointless and quite irrational because I didn't choose to be this way and it isn't my fault or anybody else's. I have often thought, *Why me?* Why did I have to be the one in 300 and, as a woman with AS, a minority within a minority group? I have always felt myself to be so abnormal as to not be really human. It is difficult for me to see myself as a person. I now think that is because I don't feel a human-to-human connection with other people, and that makes it hard for me to feel like part of the human race. And although I don't believe that it should be something to be ashamed of, I do feel ashamed of the way that I come across to other people. I am an embarrassment to myself because everyone can see my social difficulties and that extreme childlike vulnerability is so obvious to all. That is, in itself, sufficient reason for me to want to avoid social contact. I realize that there are different kinds of self-esteem. I can feel so much better about myself when I am alone, more normal even because then my social difficulties don't matter. And the more I retreat into my own world, the harder communication becomes. I have an autism outreach worker who works with me for one half day a week and we have started going to a fashion jewellery making class. I also go to a weekly art class. That at least gets me into a room with other people. I am in touch with a support service that has been set up in my area for adults who have AS.

And yet I would not want to be 'normalized'. If I had been offered a 'cure' twenty years ago, (although I had never heard of AS then and didn't know that I have it) I would probably have jumped at the chance to be 'normal' and to be free of the difficulties that I had in my life. But now I would rather just be me. My Asperger syndrome is so much a part of me that to be without it would be unthinkable. To take it away would mean, in effect, that I would become somebody else and I wouldn't now want that. To take away my AS would rob me of myself; of my private world, of my uniqueness, which I am learning to like, and it would possibly rob me of a lot of my creativity. Through counselling I came to see that all of me doesn't hate all of me, in fact there are bits of me that I like. It is my self-image in relation to other people that I don't like. Through counselling I also gained enough insight, and perhaps just enough self-confidence to begin to question whether I really wanted to change; to become more talkative, more outgoing and more sociable. And the answer is no, because that just isn't me. Even before I knew that such a thing as Asperger syndrome existed, I think I would have shouted from the rooftops for my right to be me, that is if I wasn't so inhibited about using my voice. I am not a people person and am generally happiest when I am on my own. It is reassuring for me to be where civilization is and to know that people are accessible, but I don't feel the need for social contact and I don't desire it because I find it so difficult and so uncomfortable. In social situations I feel lost. I also feel conspicuous and self-conscious because I will most likely be the only person sitting on my own and not talking to anyone. At the same time I dread the prospect of somebody coming along and trying to make small talk with me. I now avoid such situations as far as I possibly can because I come away from those occasions feeling very upset and it can take me several days to start to feel better about myself again.

When I was younger I keenly felt the absence of friendships from my life and I felt very lonely most of the time. Social isolation has sometimes been one of the hardest things for me to cope with, and far from being a consequence of my depression; it has at times been a major cause of depression for me. Through having so much counselling over the years, I think I have learned how to be my own therapist. If I am feeling traumatized by events in my life I am inclined to take it into my plastic bubble, into my own private world and deal with it in there, alone, rather than looking to anybody else for support. Feeling emotions and expressing them is something that I can only do on my own. I can only talk to other people about my feelings or about things that are happening in my life in a very objective and unemotional way. I find the presence of other people to be inhibiting, and it is only when I am alone that I can feel free to be myself. I am learning to be all of the things to and for myself that other people might typically look to one another for; therapist, mentor, mother and, above all, a friend to myself, even though I get really mad at myself sometimes. I hardly ever feel lonely now, even though I am as socially isolated as I ever was. Having my young son in my life has helped, but I enjoy my own company so much now that I can't get enough of it.

Chapter 13

The Art of Being Content: Asperger Syndrome, Buddhism and Me

Chris Mitchell

Introduction by Luke Beardon

Chris writes an interesting chapter based on how the teachings of others can influence thought processes and assist in identifying what is and is not important when it comes to being content with oneself. Life can often seem unfair, in all walks of life. It is not unreasonable to suggest that many people with AS have to deal with more unfairness in their lives compared to much of the population, and how to deal with such levels of imbalance is an extremely important point, and one which I suspect is not addressed in anywhere near as much detail as it needs to be for many people. There are numerous 'programmes' for people with AS (though with varying degrees of 'success') but it strikes me that many (most?) of these are aimed at somehow changing the behaviour of the individual – social skills programmes, anger management, and so on. I am not suggesting that these are not beneficial in any way – for some people I am sure they can be very useful – but I am also aware that there are very few (if any?) good programmes for people with AS to assist in how to cope with the lack of justice in the world and other such areas of huge importance to so many with AS. I suspect that the programmes often developed are done so from the perspective of the NT population in terms of what may benefit those with AS – but rarely, if ever, are support systems put in place that have stemmed directly from the population of people with AS themselves. This merely adds to the notion that life, for many with AS, is deeply unfair.

As a person with Asperger syndrome, I have experienced depression, high-level anxiety and obsessive-ness, all of which affect my state of mind, to the extent that I can lose my relationship with my immediate surroundings and forget who I am. For the past four years at the time of writing, I have been practising Samatha meditation, which has made a difference, opening up the untapped abilities of my mind.

Frustration (*dukkha*) creeps into me every day, in many different forms. While I feel insular, like a seed frozen in time, people around me are moving on with their lives both professionally, through being promoted at work and earning high salaries and socially, making high-profile contacts through networking, developing relationships before getting married and starting families and getting onto the property ladder. Such transitions among people around my age are common topics of conversation to which I can't relate, resulting in social isolation and low self-esteem.

It is very easy for me to be distracted by what the Buddha described as the root of all suffering, desire. Hearing about how people around my age are making professional and social progress can sometimes make me feel rather inadequate. When an undergraduate university student, I often used to feel isolated from career-minded individuals. Now, when at work or social events, where topics of conversation are often about going in for higher grade jobs, who's getting married, families, etc., together with *dukkha* I feel in terms of my own personal circumstances and in terms of being educated to MA (Hons) level but doing a basic clerical job that a GCSE school leaver would normally do, all this can make me feel that there are many things missing from my life.

However, when thinking about issues that people who have in life what I don't and problems often associated with such responsibilities, such as stress and anxiety, two conditions I struggle with, it then makes sense for me to feel happier without what other people around me have. For if my life was to become more stress- and anxiety-driven as well as unpredictable, I would not be happy. However lacking in ambition this may sound, personal happiness and contentment is more important to me than money and status, like Siddharta Gautama was much happier without the life of luxury and princely status he was brought up in.

Health is the most precious gain and contentment the greatest wealth.
The Dhamma, Chapter 15 Happiness, Verse 204

Throughout my life, I have found myself in many environments where individuals are fighting for position, often at the expense of others, including myself. This can lead to feelings of insecurity, uncertainty and generally low self-esteem, which in turn can lead to personal conflict. Even now, I still sometimes find myself in situations where 'social hierarchy' is visible, in terms of where different people are able to discuss issues that they are 'socially qualified' to talk about, be it office politics, working relations, weddings, etc.

The Buddha's teachings suggest that desire can be a fetter stronger than iron, wood or hemp. Personally, I feel that in addition to being a fetter, desire can be a source of unhappiness. Though it is often within human nature to want to own material possessions, acquire status and generally achieve goals and ambitions by whatever means, attachment to such desires can not only be a fetter, but a source of frustration, particularly if the individual finds that they can't live up to such high expectations, mentally and temperamentally, and find themselves becoming 'frustrated ghosts'.

With many material possessions or status, one can find that there is a limited period of happiness associated with them and rarely is there longevity. For instance, when one buys a new jewel, ornament, electronic gadget, item of clothing, etc. that our peers or various advertisements say is the 'in thing' to have, sometimes even implying that you are not 'one of us' if you don't have the possessions and status we have. But when the material item that one acquires suddenly isn't fashionable any more or has been replaced by something technologically advanced, the happiness that the item initially brought disappears and is replaced by frustration (*dukkah*).

Since being diagnosed with Asperger syndrome, one of the most important personal issues I feel that I have learned in this sense is to look at what I do, whether I do it successfully or unsuccessfully, on how it reflects on me or how good an achievement it is for me, being as positive as I possibly can, even in failure. For instance, when I was at university it often used to be the case where I felt so inferior to my peers when I couldn't get grades as good on paper as theirs however much work I felt I had put in. It is easy for me to feel this way now, when at work there are people so many salary scales above me who have far less education than I have. Since though, I have learned to look at whatever I attain as how good it is for me in regard to my circumstances in the sense that I was able to attain grades acceptable to university standards after years of needing extra help with some subject at school just to enter higher education.

As said in the Dhammapada, the mind is 'fickle and flighty', like a monkey. It is up to the individual to control it effectively. The tools required to control the mind through meditation, including right effort and application, can also have beneficial effects to one's quality of life in terms of being able to effectively recognise sources of suffering as well as becoming more skilled socially. These are aspects of life that as a person diagnosed with Asperger syndrome I have also had difficulties with.

The abilities of my mind I have begun to realise are those that I often experienced difficulty with relating to my Asperger syndrome, including flexibility of thought and being able to recognise reasoning for actions of others, as well as the roots of my own states of mind from anger to excitement. This, I feel has increased my awareness of myself to the extent that I can recognise the roots of low self-esteem I often experience. This enables me to deal with these issues better, helping my quality of life in terms of self-esteem.

Being diagnosed with Asperger syndrome, I really like being the way I am, particularly in regard to some of the characteristics and even abilities that the condition enables. I wouldn't accept a cure for my condition if it ever became available, or ever deny it, as this would distance me from truth. Development of mindfulness through meditation has enabled me to be a person with Asperger syndrome, while simultaneously helping me to become more aware and tolerant of my surroundings. Ultimately though, while I am alive, my goal in life is generally to achieve contentment and well-being.

Chapter 14

A Journey Looking for Answers About the Way I Am

Anthony Sclafani

Introduction by Luke Beardon

It is clear on reading this that issues for people with AS are not constrained by geographical boundaries – many of the issues raised by Anthony here are similar in nature to those experienced by people with AS all over the globe. One of the critical areas that leaps out on reading Anthony's article is just how crucial individual professionals are when it comes to providing support. It is not the name or title of the profession that is of importance when it comes to support, it is the ability of that individual that is of prime importance. Anthony, it would seem, has not had a great deal of successful input from professionals – a similar story for many with AS. Personally, I do not believe that there is an automatic understanding of AS in any profession – simply being a counsellor or psychologist, for example, does not mean that the professional in question will have a good understanding of AS or how to best support an individual with AS. I have always supported the notion that autism/AS should be a discipline in its own right; it would not solve all problems overnight, but it should reduce the damage that can be done by professionals who lack the necessary 'qualities and qualifications' to best support people with AS.

I'm a 33-year-old male from New York City, USA who was diagnosed with Asperger syndrome back in November 2001. For experiences with mental health I have to go back to my past when I was a child and work my way forward.

When I was around four years old I did not speak, I seemed to be in another world, I tended to have occasional tantrums, and I had odd mannerisms and did not really exhibit any eye contact towards people. My parents at the time knew something was wrong. They took me to the doctor and he referred us to a hospital that did special testing on children with various problems. At the hospital we saw many different types of specialists (psychologists, psychiatrists, social workers, neurologists…) and they all tested me. Believe it or not, at the time they could not really come up with any specific diagnosis for my problems. They simply stated I was 'atypical', had emotional problems and was near-sighted. Many of the specialists over there did admit that I exhibited autistic traits but never diagnosed me as such for whatever reason. Even though the diagnosis was shaky they told my parents that I could not go to regular school but had to go to special ed school for kids similar to me. My parents did attempt to bring me to a number of other specialists for a second opinion but the result was pretty much the same. As time went on I did end up in a special ed school for kids similar to me.

During the first eight years of my schooling I attended a small special school for children similar to me. While at the school I grew, developed, matured and even had some low points. This school also did some testing on me on and off during the years I was there. There was one point when I was there that the school felt I had a learning disability and needed to be put on Ritalin. I was on Ritalin for a few days but it did not help at all! Ritalin made things worse for me. My parents went to the school to complain about the trouble Ritalin was causing, and the school immediately took me off of it. When I was on Ritalin I was like a zombie, really out of it. During the rest of my eight years I was not put on any more medication. I did see a psychologist for a number of years there, even a psychiatrist for a while. Most of the time I was there I saw social workers who provided the bulk of the counseling. The social workers, for the most part, did assist me in many of my problems. The classes there were very small and the teachers not only taught subjects they also helped students with their problems and observed their behavior so they can report any changes (good or bad) to the key people. I also had to see a number of speech therapists there. They helped me to talk and to speak correctly. It was not easy learning how to talk when you're around five years old and then learning to speak correctly after learning how to talk so late. As I learned how to talk, understand my surroundings better and even learn how to deal with my peer group, things actually changed a bit for the better and to some extent for the worse. On the positive side I had the ability to communicate with people, got out of my shell a tiny bit, but on the negative side I developed a number of phobias. Socializing with my peer group was still a major hurdle for me, and I started to get into a number of things that children my age did not have any interest for (bus schedules, maps, certain historical events, causes of fires, years of cars and when things were built). Even though my eight years in this school helped me a lot, there still was a long way to go for me.

After the eight years of being in a small special ed school I graduated there and ended up in a special ed program at a large urban junior high school. I was there two years. The change from a small structured settlement into this chaos was unbelievable. My two years in this place changed me forever! I became more paranoid, more self-conscious, had even more difficulty with my peer group, became overwhelmed with the amount of students and became more sensitive. The reason for all of this was because I was teased, disrespected, ostracized and abused by the students in that place. Even my fellow students in my special ed program did not treat me properly. I won't get into the details of what happened with me and these students, but it was not good and really put an impression on me to this day. I was in the special ed program at this school for most of the two years there. While in the special ed program I still did speech therapy and had counseling. The speech therapy did not really do that much since most of the work was done to some extent. The counseling was okay but it did not really help me get through and deal with my fellow students and their abuse. As I spent my two years there I gradually mainstreamed into regular education. Towards the last few months I was fully mainstreamed into regular education. Even when I was fully mainstreamed into regular education I still went to counseling and even went to resource room to help me with my studies, especially with math (which was my weak subject at the time). Despite the horror during these two years I did manage to get along with a few of my fellow students pretty well, believe it or not, I did manage to get used to the way things worked in that school and was highly respected by my teachers for my course work and coming a long way during the last few years.

After the two years of torture I was able to get into a smaller and private high school. The experience over there was much better, even though things were far from perfect. For a while I did not go for any counseling or therapy. The counseling and therapy during this time started towards the end of my four-year tenure in this high school. I did see a guidance counselor over there. Even though he did try to help me with some of my personal challenges, the focus was helping figure what I wanted to do with myself after high school and to try to help me with my fear of going to college. I also saw a social worker outside of the school during this time. The social worker was the one who tried to help me with my personal problems. This social worker I went to was a waste! All he wanted to do was to play games and charge very high fees. He really did not say much or do anything. He felt I did not trust him and tried to get me to go against my parents. The whole brief experience was a bit odd and disappointing. We managed to find another social worker in a mental health agency. At this mental health agency I was evaluated. The psychiatrist over there could not really give me a firm diagnosis either. He did agree I had some problems but was surprised that I was in such a structured area of special education years back. The psychiatrist over there referred me to the social worker. I went to the social worker over there for a brief time. This man tried to help me but it was a bit wasteful also. Nothing came out of it, and he seemed to talk on a higher level which I could not properly comprehend too well. I eventually stopped seeing him.

After high school I did manage to go to college. I went to college for about five years and did graduate with a degree. It was truly amazing that I was able to handle college. I thought I was never going to do it but I did it. When I was at college I became exposed to many things. I learned to be a little more independent, do things on my own, take a little more initiative, actually learned on my own to deal with fellow students there and started focusing on my future. Even at college I did see a number of counselors there including a psychologist for academic and personal counseling. I did enroll in a special group over there that helped students with various personal issues and challenges. This group did help me in a number of ways. I was able to register early, I got to know students who were somewhat similar to me, got more personalized counseling and was eligible for other services as needed. The counselors and psychologist did their best to guide me through college and even assisted me with personal issues. One situation that changed me over there was I developed a crush on a fellow female student. I won't get into details of this but during this period and afterwards I was in pretty bad shape mentally and emotionally. I was obsessed, depressed, I had all kinds of weird feelings and thoughts about the whole matter, I was melancholy and this whole experience changed my thought pattern. During this time the psychologist tried to help me deal with this. The help that was provided did guide and aid me a bit, but time was the assistance in getting through this situation. It took me until I graduated to get through this situation. Towards the end of my college tenure I needed counseling in figuring out what to do with myself. Long story short: I did graduate but I ended up getting a job instead. I was not ready for graduate school, really did not know what I wanted to do with myself and I became so adjusted to the routine of going to college, taking the classes and even meeting different people that it was hard to break this mold.

A number of years ago my dad was reading an article about Asperger syndrome in a magazine. He showed me the article and stated that I had most of the symptoms in some way or another. I looked over the article and decided to research this a little bit more. I found a psychiatrist that specialized in Asperger syndrome. I went to him and he did agree that I had a very mild form of Asperger syndrome. He said I was pretty unique in the sense that I was actually very high-functioning in comparison to the other Aspies that he dealt with. He thought about giving me some medication for my anxiety and depression but felt it was not necessary at the time. He advised me to look into groups for people with Asperger syndrome. I did and found a couple. I went to them and sadly could not fit in. Even though I was very similar to many of these fellow Aspies and I was so different at the same time! At this point, since I finally got a computer with internet access, I decided to make an AS group of my own. I was able to relate a little bit more to some of the members of my group than to the members of other Aspie groups that I went to.

Right now I'm not going to any counseling or therapy. Whether I should or not is another story. Even though I have a diagnosis of Asperger syndrome, to some extent I still occasionally look for other outlets of diagnosis since not much came of the diagnosis provided by the specialist who diagnosed me. I did buy a special program for anxiety and depression a few years ago. It's a comprehensive program and it did aid in some ways. It gave me tips on how to handle my anxiety, think more positively and deal with any panic attack issues. I also take St John's wort and a mixture of melissa leaf/lemon balm/ passion leaf for my anxiety and depression. They do help a little. All that I can say is have an open mind, try to be positive as much as you can (easier said than done), learn about the world as much as you can, ask for help when needed and try to observe your surroundings more carefully.

Chapter 15

A Label that Fits: Diagnoses, Self-harm and Mental Health

Natasha Goldthorpe

Introduction by Luke Beardon

This is one of the most powerful pieces of writing in terms of putting forward an argument pro-diagnosis. The impact that the diagnosis has had on Natasha is clear and extraordinary. This does not mean that every single person with AS should get a diagnosis, nor that all people will find it a positive experience — what it does suggest, however, is that people like Natasha should never have to suffer in the way that Natasha has had to, as a result of not getting a diagnosis at an earlier age. Diagnostic processes continue to improve, and as a result the number of people getting a diagnosis is increasing. There is a long way to go, but at least the direction is the right one.

This article is written by an extraordinary individual with a strength of will that is clear in her writing. Her story is a powerful one and one which contains many lessons. One of the most important lessons for me, however, is that while Natasha's experiences are traumatic and devastating, she is by no means alone in them. That anyone should have to go through such experiences is a travesty. While services are slowly improving there must be no stopping until experiences such as Natasha's are firmly in the past, never to be repeated.

Often when I tell people I have Asperger syndrome they say they would never have guessed or look at me in complete disbelief; I'm 'too sociable', I can have conversations, I sing in pubs and drink beer, I have a boyfriend, two jobs and live independently with my dog, cat and fish. The truth is the reason I can do all this – and more – and appear so 'normal' is due to my diagnosis and the sense it enabled me to make out of myself, my life and the world around me. I think it is only the people who have known me since before my diagnosis, the ones who never gave up on me and struggled to live with me, who can fully appreciate the dramatic changes the diagnosis made. Looking back at myself, as little as six years ago, I find it difficult to visualise the girl who was sinking in a swamp of psychiatric labels with a trail of hospital admissions behind her and was told she needed to go and live in a care home.

I found a website on Asperger syndrome online by accident, aged 22, while searching for clues about my various obsessive behaviours. I'd been sitting in my bedroom for a couple of months, which was nothing out of the ordinary for me then, having a fear of, and no reason for, leaving the house. I hadn't finished reading the article before I could hardly focus on the words upon words describing me. I immediately scoured the internet and library for all the information I could find on Asperger syndrome, I was expecting, or perhaps looking, for a statement that would prove me wrong and would conclude this to be yet another label that 'does not quite fit', but the more I read, the more I related and the more elated, angry, sad and, mostly, relieved I felt in huge waves of emotion that literally made me shake. The personal stories of people I didn't know described me down to the tiniest details and I was able to connect myself suddenly to the external world and, in a sharp jolt, to my body.

During my last hospital admission of seven months I had medical books at my fingertips and read them avidly. Partly motivated by my hopeless-seeming quest to find out what was wrong with me and partly from the fact that medical lists had become an unhealthy but intense interest. I could quote from the BNF, DSM-IV, ICD-10 and even surgical nursing dictionaries as well as knowing the names, uses and dosage guidelines of most psychiatric drugs. However close any diagnosis came to describing me though, however much I latched on to and explored it, hoping it would help me, it would only lead me to yet another dead end. Certain labels did fit my periods of depressive, anxious, and, less often, psychotic episodes, and these were the labels used by doctors in my treatment. But these were all secondary to my main concern; that I was 'wrong' whether I was ill or not, that my core self was defective or, even worse, not there at all.

I have never felt such profound feelings of clarity and enlightenment in my life as during those first three days of solid reading about Asperger syndrome. I saw my whole life from a different perspective. It was as though I'd been walking through a room unable to find the exit, tripping up, falling and bumping into big obstacles until I was bruised and exhausted. I'd come to a wall and unsteadily edged my way along it hoping to find a way out only to trip again, accidently catching a lever which I'd pulled down. Suddenly I can see! A light has come on which no one told me was there. The obstacles are still there but now I can attach names and colours and shapes to them and the whole room is quite a fascinating place. So I forget about the exit for a while and decide to stay and have a look round!

I was formally diagnosed when I was 23 after a year-long uphill struggle to get my psychiatrist to refer me to someone who had the training to recognise that I was on the autistic spectrum. During that year I almost gave up on pursuing the formal diagnosis because it was using up so much of my energy. I deeply resented the fact that I had to see yet another professional, especially one I didn't know, to validate who I am and was anxiously anticipating the psychologist disagreeing with me and saying I don't have Asperger syndrome. To me that would be like someone telling a gay person that they aren't gay. I persevered for formal diagnosis, not for anyone else, not because I needed someone to tell me what I was, or even in order to get support, but for closure of a lifetime of bewilderment.

It terrifies me to think where I might be now if I hadn't found that website. At the next meeting with my psychiatrist, after several meetings with a clinical psychologist who assessed me and confirmed the diagnosis, I was discharged from the mental health system. I walked out of the building feeling so vulnerable having spent the previous six years under the care of various mental health professionals. I also felt free and determined to turn my life around. The research I had already done on Asperger's had given me insight into my problems in the past and the confidence to face the future armed with self-knowledge and, a feeling completely alien to me, a huge passion for living. Perhaps the main thing I gained from my diagnosis was a sense of self; the gaping empty universe inside my shell of a body was filled up.

My mental health problems had crept up gradually while I was at boarding school. I was a smiley, jokey person and once even got a certificate for having the 'biggest smile'. Under the smile, though, I was becoming increasingly anxious and confused about my growing realisation and overwhelming feeling that I didn't belong. My GCSE year came as a short relief; I threw myself into the school musical and my art GCSE. I had an intense passion for drama and spent the few non-rehearsal evenings up in the art studio painting fish. I was too involved in my activities to address the crushing waves of negative feelings that I couldn't work out at the time. During the summer that followed, without the structure and busyness of school to keep me occupied, I began focusing in to an extreme on imperfections in my environment that I couldn't stop myself from noticing and becoming obsessive about them as a way, I think, of avoiding those feelings and to somehow anchor me to the physical world, including my own body, that I felt I was drifting away from. I spent that summer holiday furiously vacuuming lumps out of my bedroom carpet for around four hours a day, cleaning and tidying the kitchen over and over again, washing cutlery and sideboards while my family were still using them. I slept as much as I could to escape having to go through the motions of being alive.

I was known to be prone to rages and rapid mood swings at school but during sixth form my moods began swinging more chaotically than ever. One minute I could be laughing hysterically at something I found funny, the next I could be storming out of lessons in a rage, my behaviour was completely erratic. I was, and still am, extra sensitive to my environment, slight changes to lesson timetables confused my whole day, sudden loud noises cause me to scream and panic internally although I rarely express this outwardly, natural and fluorescent lighting is painful on my eyes. As a privilege, being sixth-formers, some of our lessons were taken in the lounge of the sixth-form house on expensive new sofas. I hated this. I hated the fact there were no desks to write on and that our bedrooms were only upstairs, there was no distinction any more between the school day and free time. I would go off for long walks on my own wondering and worrying about why I felt so different to the girls who I'd lived with for the last nine years, growing lonelier and more alien to myself and everyone else. The smile that had been stuck to my face for 17 years gradually disappeared. I appeared disruptive, angry and rude but most of the time I was not intending to be. I was gradually just slipping further and further behind a thick screen that separated me from everyone and everything else, I just could not connect. I was nominated drama rep and took my job so seriously that it became more important than my lessons, it gave me a reason to get out of bed each day. I found temporary comfort each day watching the washing machine's whirling circles and could only even attempt homework at night when everyone else was asleep. My remaining time at school was spent drifting aimlessly around the buildings, washing and rewashing my clothes and bed linen and lying in my room wishing as hard as I could that I would die in my sleep.

My parents were informed I was suicidal and that there was 'something different about me' and came to try and persuade me to come home for a bit. My resistance and anxiety over any type of transition was the reason I stayed at school. I even tried to stay there during the holidays but wasn't allowed. Other girls' parents warned their daughters not to hang around with me as I was a bad influence. Half way through the year I was suspended for drinking and, as a result, banned from boarding. As a day-girl I would become practically mute every evening from the moment the bus dropped me off and I got in the car. It wasn't that I didn't want to speak or I was being actively antagonistic or trying to upset anyone. I was confused by vague questions like 'How was your day?' and couldn't think of an answer or I thought of hundreds of answers and didn't know which to say. Trying to transpose answers into spoken words needed energy, I had used up all my energy at school trying as hard as I could to appear normal and stand up for myself against what seemed like an increasingly threatening and muddling environment. Sometimes I did, eventually, manage to form the words in my head, but they would shrink back and get lost on the way to my mouth and I would just stare ahead thinking about this, feeling as though, like my words, I was shrinking back further and further in to my shell of a body, but it felt calmer and safer the more I withdrew. Inside it was silent and words couldn't reach me or tie me up, I could just float. Before I began to use this regularly as a coping mechanism I would reach the point where the images in my head would burst out in an explosion of uncontrolled and incomprehensible emotion, like a fizzed up coke bottle I'd just burst, screaming, crying, smacking and punching myself. As I got older I found myself pulling my anger inwards more and more rather than letting it out, 'sliding backwards and upwards' into my shell, into a space of silence, all external noise and sensations blocked out. At the same time I didn't feel as if my body was attached to me, it was more of a shell that I was a temporary inhabitant of, like a hermit crab. My feelings of being an outsider, detached from the world became more powerful than ever. I tried explaining this to a psychotherapist by drawing myself as an astronaut, floating in space, holding a broken cord that should have been attached to a rocket, not able to use my body to signal to the people inside the rocket who were smiling out, unaware I was drifting further and further into space.

I left school at 17 and made a very rushed move to drama school in London. I auditioned, got a place and moved to London all within two weeks fuelled by my determination and nervous energy. I managed three months there in a zombie-like state, unable to focus on learning lines, unable to pay attention in the classes and had a breakdown. I spent the next couple of years in my bedroom back at my parents' house, sleeping all day and lying awake at night. I could not stand the confusion and noise of daytime outside my window, the cars and people. Gradually I began to get up at night and started listening to certain CDs on loop and drew tiny intricate pictures of sea animals and mythical creatures, printing out hundreds of pictures of unicorns and fairies to stick on my walls. I read the whole of the Encarta encyclopaedia on the computer the rest of the time. When I wasn't drawing or reading I felt hollow and lonely and as though I was about to disappear, I constantly visualised the room melting around me and the only way of trying to explain things to myself then was to write poetry. I began to deeply question myself and my existence and the existence of the world outside, leading me later on to courses in philosophy of mind and became fascinated by solipsism. I was so separate from anything happening outside my room, or in fact my body, it was easy to believe none of it was really there and I was alone.

When I was 19, my parents eventually, after much hard work, got me to a doctor. I was referred to a psychiatrist who diagnosed me with bipolar disorder, put me on lithium and admitted me to hospital shortly afterwards, where I stayed for two months. This was the first of seven admissions in which I went through so many medication changes I lost count. For the next few years I was trapped in that hospital's revolving door, a voluntary patient at first and then several Sections, and pumped with psychiatric drugs until my mind felt like a constant cloud. The side effects I experienced were intense, I am hypersensitive to medication, but when I tried explaining this I either wasn't believed or told that I was exaggerating. I spent one admission sucking liquid meals out of a straw in bed because I didn't have the strength to eat; my head had fallen into my food on several occasions. One strong, old type of antipsychotic caused my limbs and neck to stiffen and twist until I could not walk; it caused my jaw to tense up and my leg to drag behind me like in pictures of 19th-century asylums, most antipsychotics just made me feel continually exhausted.

As my leave was being discussed at a meeting, a locum doctor once said to me I must look at him while he's speaking to me. I didn't look at him. Then he asked again and I still didn't look at him. Then he said he would Section me if I did not look at him. So I was forced to look at him and then I couldn't concentrate on what he was saying.

I left hospital and moved in to a house near my parents and stopped taking my medication. I was, and still am, strongly against taking medication.

My lack of friends was painfully obvious to me, especially on my birthdays. I watched groups of students walking to and from college outside my window wishing I could be part of their groups. I began researching college courses for this reason, joining an adult education class for two hours a week. Within weeks I was an expert on every single course on offer in Norfolk at every venue, plus I had memorised every Open University course code inadvertently while reading course descriptions on their website. My bedtime reading were prospectuses and medical directories, and I sometimes went without sleep to read more, winding myself up with a kind of anxious excitement and constant obsessive planning, re-planning and timelines, mapping out my future of learning. The pile of prospectuses grew, and only eight years later did I build up the courage to throw them out!

Alongside courses, I had acquired interests in nutrition, diseases and medicines. My interest in nutrition may or may not have been connected to an eating disorder that I developed in hospital which painfully dominated my life for about two years, trapping me in a cycle of obsessive thoughts and ritualistic behaviours surrounding my phobia of food that I felt I couldn't escape from on my own. I begged to be referred to the eating disorders clinic, and my family supported me in this. I visited the clinic and met the nurses, I wanted to get better so much but my psychiatrist would not refer me because I was 'too disturbed'. I have been recovered for a few years and generally a very healthy eater, no one would guess I am still quite obsessional over food unless they lived with me. My interest in pathology and disease worked its way into a six-week phase of mania I fell into while painting 24 hours a day for 12 days with no sleep or food (I had suddenly decided to become an art therapist and needed a portfolio for my foundation course interview). I became psychotic for the next few weeks and my delusions and hallucinations were all based around extreme and 'undiscovered diseases' in which my muscles turned into chewing gum and my face melted into wax while I was doing a self-portrait in the mirror among other things. This was a terrifying experience and no one could talk me out of my beliefs. I did create a huge portfolio of art though, which got me a place on an art foundation course. I snapped out of this episode while painting my living room emerald green. Colours have a huge effect on me, both positively and negatively. The last interest, medicine, was the most dangerous of all. I had a phobia of taking psychiatric medication; maybe because I'd been on so many tablets, injected against my will and because I felt they weren't addressing my main problems. However much I avoided taking them though, I read all the labels over and over again, I hoarded them, I liked the look of bright little pills, I loved the words 'tablet' and 'chemist' and was unable to part with my collection. They felt like some kind of security while they were stashed. Although I couldn't stand taking them 'as directed', I began reaching for them every time my emotions crept up on me; I reached for a handful, then two handfuls. It was a form of self-harm, self-poisoning, that I hadn't intended to happen. It numbed me for a while. Sometimes nothing would happen and sometimes I would be sent to the general hospital for observation. When the handfuls got bigger I would be put on a drip and be flushed out. I could not stop doing it, even though I could not stand being tied up to a bed on a drip, doing everything I could to escape, including nibbling through the cord on my drip. It was only once that I took the tablets in a different way, chaotically planned but not impulsive, this was when I was 22 and attempted to take my life. My body began shutting down around me and I became a horizontal statue in my bed. I could not grasp the fact that the stone body around me actually belonged to me. I was sent back to the psychiatric hospital when I could connect to my body enough to move and then moved out back into my parents' house.

Since my diagnosis my quality of life has improved dramatically. The world makes so much more sense now that I can see and understand my difficulties. My Asperger's is with me every minute of every day and I wouldn't have it any other way, it has many great advantages and is an integral part of my identity. It is also always going to be very challenging; I want to be part of the world but I work so hard on appearing 'normal', and am so adept at it now that can be detrimental to me as it is not obvious to other people what I find difficult, what I cannot tolerate and what makes my anxiety bubble away rapidly inside. This can cause me extreme stress and to regress to old, maladaptive responses fuelled by 'fight or flight' if I don't recognise when it's happening. I cannot sustain my sociable persona before becoming completely exhausted and having to isolate myself in order to recharge and, as I know this, I can take valuable time out before I become drained and my stress levels tip over into both mental and physical health problems. I am recovered from my mental health problems now and believe they only came about because of the constant overload of sensory information and social situations that I couldn't understand or process, causing me to have to breakdown to the extreme in order to shut everything out. To remain mentally grounded I believe that although I have chosen to adapt in some areas, the key is to not break myself in order to fit in, to know when to say 'that's enough'. I'm always going to have high stress levels because of the environments I put myself in and the pressures I put upon myself, but they are choices I make and I now thrive on the challenges that make me feel alive. I don't look back with regret or bitterness any more, but use my experiences in the most positive way I can to support others with Asperger syndrome.

Chapter 16

Through the Looking Glass into Lynette Land: Making Humour Work

Lynette Marshall

Dedicated to my special friend Ryan Bramwell.
You always made me smile. Forever with us.

Introduction by Luke Beardon

It's sometimes difficult with Lynette to remember that she has had to struggle considerably in her life and that she continues to face daily obstacles that affect her greatly; her willingness to share her optimism, her quick sense of humour, her spark for life all contribute to make for an individual for whom mental health issues are rarely discernible. However, the lack of obvious presentation does not mean in any sense that she has not suffered – time and again – from a lack of understanding of her AS and at the hands of those willing to exploit her vulnerable nature. That Lynette is able to still focus on the positives in life, and fight on, is admirable to say the least.

It is also very interesting to note the high levels of sympathy and need to help other people as much as she can that is included in Lynette's writing. Despite having all sorts of issues to deal with herself she continues to spend much of her time trying to help other people – which was in fact a major reason for her writing this chapter. Lynette is a fine example of a person with AS who destroys the stereotype of an uncaring, 'cold' person, that is sometimes portrayed in books and in the media. She is living proof that such a stereotype is a complete and utter nonsense.

Those who know me know me to be a happy person, perhaps with a rather 'different' sense of humour. Friends come to expect that a good 80 per cent of my communication with them is through jokes; I am forever the joker and love nothing better than a good laugh. When Luke approached me to ask if I would contribute to a book about Asperger's and mental health can you guess what I did? Yes, I laughed. I laughed because as a fun-loving person I do not find it easy to discuss mental health issues nor do I like thinking negatively. After greater thought I realised how important mental well being is to any person either with Asperger's (AS), autistic or neurotypical (NT). If any of what I write supports or helps one person then it has been worthwhile.

Issues with mental health, for example depression, anxiety and obsessional thoughts, often appear to occur alongside AS. Do any of you NTs feel anxious about sitting an exam? Or taking a driving test? People with AS may feel anxious about things you may think are trivial, for example changing to a new toothbrush, not travelling on the usual road home from school. Do any of you NTs ever feel depressed? When a relationship comes to an end, for example. I feel that one big reason why people with AS become depressed is due to communication. Imagine living in a world where few people really understood you. When you are trying to be polite and friendly and others think you are rude. Imagine the isolation when being segregated from a group due to wearing clothes that do not colour-coordinate. What a frustrating world! It was through greater thought that I realised that I had been affected by mental health issues that are simply due to my having AS and living in a world that is mostly populated by NTs and the lack of understanding that sometimes causes.

Ironically, before being diagnosed with AS, for many years professionals thought I was clinically depressed. I was prescribed medication. If nothing improved the dose was increased or the medication was changed. The solution was not this simple. Whilst I do believe that medication can be useful and effective for some people, the onus should not just be on us to take our medication. Training needs to be undertaken regarding the autism spectrum. Awareness of AS and autism needs to be raised. For any interaction to take place at least two people need to be involved in it. Can any of you NTs imagine a world where most people in most of the interactions that you engage in do not speak to you in a way that you understand? It is quite normal for people with AS not to understand what you have said, what you are asking us to do and how best we should respond to you. This is the fault of nobody, but if you could learn how to give us clear and short instructions, be clear and follow through with what you say and give us some thinking time to respond to you, then you will help us greatly to understand the conversation and develop our social skills. It is my feeling that when a conversation fails or a friendship fails, between an NT and a person with AS, the person with AS can take this very personally and blame themselves. This can lead to low self-esteem and depression. The person with AS may become isolated because they do not want to experience the failure again and thus a vicious circle develops of experience of a difficult social interaction leading to increased isolation leading to depression and/or low self-esteem.

People with AS have every right to participate in a social life and have similar experiences of being able to work, study and have friends as any other person. Think about if you were holding a conversation with a blind person – would you give them something to look at? If they are completely blind and you are a decent person then the answer is no. How about a person who is deaf – would you talk to them and expect them to be able to hear you? Again, if you are a decent person and the person in question has no hearing at all then you would find an alternative way of holding a conversation with them, such as signing, the use of pictures and the written word. Our difficulty as people with AS is that our disability may not be obvious to others, and thus our needs may not be met and this produces feelings of sadness. People have thought at times that I am rude because I do not answer a question straight away. The only reason that I am not answering the question straight away is that I am still thinking about what the other person has said and processing what they have said. These prejudices that we may be rude affect our confidence and self-esteem when we are basically just trying to understand you.

Note to NTs: Ask us what our difficulties are and/or spend time with us to discover what our difficulties are, listen to our responses and support us in the way that we ask for, as well as having some time for yourself!! I do understand as a support worker myself how tiring this can be! But really if you could just accept our differences and listen to us you will be doing a wonderful job! Thank you. *Note to people with AS*: You have every right to enjoy a variety of experiences and to live life to the full. Live it and enjoy it! A good tip that I have been given is to ignore the bad stuff and focus on the positive aspects of your life. I believe that everybody, regardless of if they have AS or not, experiences knocks to their confidence. Keep going, have a rest and recharge and you can succeed!!

It appears that for some people with AS low self-esteem can be an issue. People may find it difficult to interact socially and thus have a tendency to be on their own. In my experience people with AS want to make friends. They can feel low in mood if they do not have the opportunities to make friends or if they find maintaining friendships difficult and lose friends or find social situations confusing. The best way in which NTs can help us is to be supportive, spend the time to get to know us as people and explain things to us if we have not understood. Confusion can be a big cause of anxiety for us. Therefore if we can be supported with appropriate explanations, this decreases our confusion, decreases our anxiety levels and helps us along our path to mental and emotional well being. In my opinion people with AS are able to achieve a lot. They can be proud of everything that they do achieve.

I am an example of a person with AS who has achieved some of my goals in life. I have a full-time job, I have a BA (Hons) in Early Childhood Studies and I am currently studying for a Master's in Autism. I do have some very good friends. My motto is that if I can achieve these things then so can other people, with a varying level of support. I am a great believer that people with AS can be proud to have it. Having AS I believe forms part of my intelligence, it helps me to achieve my very best at work and study. I also believe that for every difficulty that AS brings there is a positive perspective to it. For instance, obsessional thoughts are often thought of as intrusive. Though being very interested in a topic can be highly beneficial. It can lead to successful careers and hobbies.

I have found an attitude to AS which seems to work well for me. That is to be realistic with regard to the difficulties that I have. But at the same time to think positively and maintain a sense of fun. If I were not realistic about what my difficulties are, I would be unable to gain the support that I need. I may also attempt to do things which are too difficult for me; and if this results in a failure, then my confidence will be knocked. But if I accept what my difficulties are, I can plan to take little steps towards achieving a goal. In taking things slowly I can progress and achieve and this gives me confidence.

Who should take responsibility for maintaining a healthy level of mental health for individuals with AS? Everybody. Professionals, family, friends and strangers – in an ideal world. Treating people with respect is very important. I do not expect NTs to understand my behaviour or why I behave differently to them. But just an acceptance that I will understand and behave differently to them would be wonderful. I have often known it to be the case that people with AS have not been given the respect that they deserve and instead are sometimes bullied. I have been the victim of bullying myself. Bullying has a negative effect on self-esteem.

Note to the bully: Are you finding fault with our difficulties? We can do that with you – you must have some difficulties since you are bullying us in the first place! Nobody likes a bully. Though I believe that you can change and become a better person. *Note to a person with AS who is being bullied*: The bully does not deserve to know you. The bullying is not your fault. Please find a trusted person to talk to. I overcame bullying. You can too!

Even receiving my diagnosis of AS raised my self-esteem. I had always known that there were some social situations that I found hard and that I felt different to how I thought that other people were. Though I had no name for how I felt. This in itself did not help as I basically started to convince myself that I was going mad. This did very little for my self-esteem. After being told I had AS I went through a short period of shock and upset. Then came a reason for my difficulties *and* my qualities, I felt relieved and I have a better sense of who I am as a person. I knew at the point of diagnosis that I was not mad. I was just different to some people, in a special way. My diagnosis was very positive for me. Up until my diagnosis I was depressed, felt 'mad' and not in control of my life. Since gaining my diagnosis I have felt confident, happy and in control of my life. I would urge anybody to view a diagnosis of AS positively. You are the same person as you always have been and there are people that love and care for you. My diagnosis came as a shock to me, since I was 25 years old and already an adult. I was being diagnosed with having difficulties, but look how well I had done to go through school, gain 'A' levels, gain a degree in Early Childhood Studies, and pass my driving test first time – all with my difficulties.

Note to people with AS: Just because you think and behave differently to NTs does not mean that you are mad. You are unique and have a refreshing way of thinking. *Note to NTs*: Because we may behave in a way which is not expected by society you may hold the misconception that we are aggressive or mean others harm. I would like to state that I do not believe people with AS as a population to be any more aggressive than any other person. Quite the opposite in fact. I find people with AS to be caring natured and if you do not have a friend with AS you are missing out!

I mentioned anxiety earlier in the chapter. Through my childhood I have been anxious about dental appointments, heights and low-flying aircraft, to name a few. If I made a weekly diary there would be occurrences of anxiety every day. I am anxious about meeting new people, attending social gatherings and trying to find a partner. I do believe though that I can learn through practice and support. Unpredictable situations can cause a great deal of anxiety to people with AS. This is why using a timetable for the day can really help. It makes life a little more predictable. In order to decrease anxiety coping strategies can be used. These have to be specific to the individual and again it is often trial and error to find the strategy that works. You are important as a person and deserve some time to relax. Whether it is having a bath, swimming, reading a book, listening to music. Find what relaxes you and regularly participate in it. Thanks to a good friend for the suggestion I now have 'me' time scheduled into every week where I can focus on doing something which solely benefits me. It reduces the stress that I feel. I have experienced ruminations in the past, where I have thought and thought about the one situation, I did not want to keep thinking like this but did not know how to stop the thoughts or decrease them. Finding a distraction or a hobby to focus on really helped my ruminations to decrease.

I do find that I am happiest when I am surrounded by people who understand AS and do not judge me. I find that humour helps to reduce my anxiety and stress levels. If I find something difficult I will often make a joke about it. In this way I can approach the matter light-heartedly, and this has a calming effect on me. I have told Luke several times how helpful he is in helping me to feel calmer and happier in a crisis. Luke helps me to put a situation into perspective and explore ways in which I could deal with it. Luke and I share a good sense of humour and this helps me to forget my troubles.

In order to cope with depression, medication could be taken and/or counselling could be sought. I have found a mixture of the two to suit me well. It has taken me some time to find a medication which suited me, which I felt had positive effects and not too many long-term side effects. It has taken me a similar amount of time to find a counsellor who I could properly talk to and trust. But I have succeeded in finding the medication and the counsellor that worked for me. Perseverance and support is the key. If one medication does not suit you, then you may have to be prepared to change medication under the guidance of your GP and/or psychiatrist. Support from your family and friends and/or a family support worker may benefit you during these difficult times.

As I have said earlier, medication is not a solution which has solved all of my difficulties. I will always have AS and I am proud of that fact. The wider issue is that it is not always the behaviour or the thinking of the person with AS that we need to focus on changing. As long as nobody is being harmed or abused in any way by the behaviours of the person with AS, then it may be very useful to observe if there is an aspect of the environment that could be changed. For example, people with AS and autism can be seekers or avoiders of the sensory environment. If a person does not like bright lights and they are dimmed within a setting, then we can enable that person to feel much happier by a simple action of turning the lights down. Similarly, challenging behaviour can occur if a person dislikes noises. This causes difficulties to the person with AS who may not feel comfortable and may feel stressed and anxious. It also causes difficulties for the surrounding people who must deal with the challenging behaviour. It is not always so easy to support a person with AS to be calm, but in this case just keeping the noise levels low could make life a lot easier for all of us. If you were scared of spiders and you walked into a room full of them crawling on the floor, would you be scared? Probably so. Would you experience symptoms of stress? For example, feeling hot, your heart beating faster, shaking? Would you feel anxious, fear for your safety and/or want to run away from the situation? I should expect so. If people with AS are asked to stay within an environment with loud noises when they don't like loud noises you are subjecting them to a similar situation as the spider situation above. If people with AS are constantly forced to make conversation this can lead to emotional exhaustion, and that could lead to stress and depression. I am all in favour of developing social skills, though I am suggesting that time and space for the person with AS to be alone and/or resting during a day can be very useful in keeping stress levels low.

When supporting a person with AS to maintain a good level of mental health I always remember to treat people as individuals. What works to make one person feel happier may not work for another person. I like to get to know a person with AS for the person that they are. Through time, I then learn what strategies tend to work for them and which do not. The qualities that I appreciate in others who are friends with me are calmness and patience and this is what I like to give to others.

I would like to state that I am amazed every day at the *abilities* that people with AS show. I am leading a happy life with AS and I would like to think that I can be an inspiration to others to feel confident about their abilities.

With many thanks to my good friend Luke Beardon. You are a star. I would not be where I am today without your wonderful support.

Note to all: Keep smiling and be happy! – Lynette xxx

Chapter 17

Mental Health and the Workplace: Dealing with Criticism, Coping with Stress, and Taking Control of Your Environment

Dr Christopher Wilson

Introduction by Luke Beardon
Christopher makes any number of important points in his chapter, but the one I think is crucial for the wider population to recognise and understand is the impact that they can have, in a negative manner, in terms of making any criticism of the person with AS. Many people do not take to criticism well – but I doubt that many suffer the consequences of ongoing rumination and mental agonising that some people with AS will undergo following criticism of their work. There may not be a simple solution to this – though in some cases it can be helpful to make it explicitly clear to the individual that criticism is meant constructively and is not meant as an overall comment on them as a person or their work as a whole. Even if there is no simple solution, at least an awareness of the very real issues that the individual may have to deal with could be beneficial to the person. I have known individuals for whom what was intended as a minor criticism has led – literally – to years of mental torture. This is the reality for some people, however difficult that is to understand. It is far too easy for

people to dismiss the problems related to criticism without truly appreciating the devastating effect it can have on the individual with AS.

Introduction

Despite suffering from both Asperger syndrome (AS) and dyslexia, my life so far has been good and I have achieved a great deal. As a child I did not have a great many friends and spent a lot of time by myself. At the time, this did not particularly bother me. Although not anti-social, I am quite happy being on my own for extended periods. Being asked to 'play out' and interact with other children often seemed like more of a chore than a pleasurable pastime. Also I was an only child and always very close to my parents. As a family, we regularly went on days out and shared a number of common interests. Most of the time, this was all the socialisation I needed or wanted.

I never enjoyed high school and, like many with AS, I was frequently left out and suffered from bullying (although with hindsight, the bullying was not nearly as bad as it could have been). Part of the problem was my unwillingness to do what was required to fit in. Like most schools, mine was 'sports mad' and so much social acceptance seemed to come from being good at (or at least showing an interest in) sport. I had no interest in sport (either watching it or playing it), yet unless you could talk football (a game I find boring beyond description), you were excluded from so much conversation. This was a particular problem in my final year when, every break and lunch, all the boys would (without fail) gather on the playing courts to play football, even those who were no good at it. But I stayed away. In my mind I had no idea why I should be forced to play a sport I hated, just to have an opportunity to socialise. I therefore spent most of my breaks in the library, where reading books was far more interesting.

It was therefore a great relief when I was able to leave school and move on to college and university. I am sure I am not the only one who has noticed how abrupt the change between school and higher education is. After 16, not only are you treated as an adult by your tutors/lecturers, but your fellow students suddenly seem capable of holding a conversation on things other than Manchester United! People also seem to lose the 'point scoring' attitude that is so much a part of teenage social interaction, i.e. the 'my dad can beat up your dad', 'I just smoked seven cigarettes' sort of boastfulness that I always found contemptible. Finally, having lectures/tutorials at regular intervals (with large breaks in between), allowed me to socialise in manageable chunks. I wasn't forced to be with people every minute of every day.

High achievement

It is no coincidence then that I was able to achieve far more at college and university, than I ever had at school – both academically and socially.

On the academic side, I left college with good A-level results, and was then able to gain first-class undergraduate and master's degrees in town planning/urban regeneration, before undertaking a PhD. Generally, my written expression is very good, although dyslexia means that I have to be extra careful about spelling and punctuation. As a diagnosed dyslexic ('statemented' was the term used then) I got extra time in exams and little stickers to put on my work, indicating I was dyslexic. Personally, I never felt I needed the latter, but was not about to turn down the extra support!

At university I also found out, to my genuine surprise, that I was quite good at giving talks, presentations and public speaking. During my PhD I was happy to give occasional lectures to students and manage seminars (i.e. assess student presentations). I found I could express myself very well in any conversation that was structured, and I had a good knowledge of the subject. It is when I am caught 'off guard' in an interaction that my verbal skills sometimes suffer.

On the social side, I was able to relate far better to my peers and make some long-term friends. Generally, I was drawn to the more intelligent, mature and hard-working members of my course, who could be both friends and useful work partners. Often these were women, although relationships remained platonic and I had few romantic encounters. Although no 'party animal' I was quite happy going for nights out, provided I knew roughly how long the night would last and when I would be back – I still like my socialisation in manageable chunks. I stayed in halls of residence for my first year as an undergrad and this allowed me to get to know my host city (Manchester) and enjoy a range of new experiences.

It was because of my success as an undergraduate that I felt able to move on and undertake a master's and PhD (the two courses were linked). Academically most of the work felt easy and unpressured, particularly for the PhD, for which I had three years to complete a single project. Although there were always things to do, I found that it only required four to six hours work per weekday to keep on schedule.

PhDs (at least in the social sciences) are usually individual projects, so you spend a lot of time by yourself, particularly when writing. This suited me fine, and what had previously been a weakness (my desire for privacy) suddenly became a strength. I was far better able to cope with the relative isolation of doing a PhD than some of the other students I knew.

After completing my PhD I decided not to continue in academia. Despite my successes, I had limited interest in the more theoretical aspects of academic work and felt that this would hold me back. I went to work for a small private consultancy firm who undertake research for local authorities and found life in the private sector very different from my previous life experiences. The work is more varied and allows me to see a lot of the UK. Although the job is generally enjoyable and my workmates are friendly, deadlines are tight and there can be a lot of pressure to get things done.

Confidence and stress

Despite my general success, a lack of confidence and low self-esteem have been issues. Although I can come across as self-assured and confident, this is not always so in my private life. I can be quite negative at times (a trait I share with my family) and have a hard time looking on the bright side when things go wrong. I also tend to brood a lot on my failures. Being a light sleeper anyway, it does not take much for me to lie awake at night and worry.

The problems in question are usually work-related. Due to my dyslexia, I make more than my fair share of minor spelling/ punctuation errors (my maths skills are also not great) and these are commented upon. I do not take criticism well and even a minor 'telling off' will affect me for days. When things do go wrong, I have a great deal of trouble telling just how much trouble I am in and whether my bosses are genuinely angry with me. This is an aspect of personal interaction that I have always struggled with. Generally, any such problems are usually short in duration – lasting no more than a week, before I can bounce back and carry on. Thankfully short-term periods of uncertainly have never become long-term depression.

Linked to this is more general stress. My job can be quite stressful, and is becoming more so as I become more senior. Although I am getting better at handling stress, it never comes naturally to me. My instinct is to do each task at a slow and steady pace, trying to be thorough and minimise any errors. Timescales do not always allow this and working at speed is never a pleasant experience.

Coping with stress and anxiety

Stress and anxiety are things we all experience from time to time. It is a normal response to situations we see as threatening to us. For example, if you had to go into hospital for an operation, sit a driving test or take an exam, it would be natural to feel anxious. Anxiety can even be helpful when we need to perform well, or cope with an emergency. However, anxiety can also be uncomfortable, frightening, and stop you from enjoying life. Based on my own personal experiences, here is some advice on how to cope with stress and anxiety.

TAKE CONTROL OF YOUR ENVIRONMENT

A lot of stress comes from the environment in which we live and work. A lot of people with AS have a sensitivity to noise or crowds, I don't, but I recognise what a problem that can be. Some difficult environments can't be avoided, but many can be. If the evening news makes you anxious, turn the TV off. Personally, I always avoid certain daily newspapers (I won't name names, but you can guess which ones) whose stories are designed to provoke anger and fear, not inform you. If traffic's got you tense, take a longer but less-travelled route. If going to the supermarket is an unpleasant chore, do your grocery shopping online.

However, it is in your own home that you will always have the most control. I don't want to be too prescriptive here; everyone has their own view on what constitutes a tidy or an untidy house. I have friends whose houses always seem a mess to me, and I have other friends who doubtless feel the same about my house. However, if the clutter of your house is causing you to lose things and be stressed, then it may be time to clean up.

It is not just about the vacuuming and the dusting though. If you are surrounded by more 'stuff' than you can manage (old DVDs, books, clothes, etc.), it sends a visual message that your life is out of control. And it can become a vicious circle, where disorder brings about procrastination, which only perpetuates the chaos.

Clearing out your clutter is easier than you think. Pick one area to tackle, such as the junk drawer in the kitchen or the piles of clothes in the bedroom. Take a hard look at what you've accumulated. Clear out any items you're not using. If they're in good condition, consider donating them to a local charity. If you absolutely can't part with some items, box them up and put an expiration date of a year in the future on the box. Store the box. If the box remains unopened until the expiration date, you clearly can do without its contents. Trash or donate the box unopened.

EXPECT THE UNEXPECTED
Other chapters in this book look at organising schedules, routines and 'to-do' lists in your daily lives. There is nothing wrong with that, we all like order in our lives and most people with AS have a strong daily/weekly routine. However, you also need to be prepared for the unexpected things life throws at you, which may require you to adapt your routine.

In my job I work for both the company's Director and Associate Director, usually undertaking separate projects for each. Generally, the two do not co-ordinate themselves well and both think what I am doing for them is more important than the tasks set by the other. Frequently I have been working on one project, only to be told that, no, I should have been working on another. Upon switching to the other project I am then told (by the other Director) that, no, I should have been working on the first project, and so on. For anybody this would be frustrating, for someone with AS it is positively agonising.

This may not be a problem you have faced, but it illustrates that no matter how perfectly you plan your day (or your life), sooner or later, other people will throw a spanner in the works and cause you stress. This applies both to your work life and social life, where people will rarely behave exactly as you want them. You will have to adapt your daily/weekly routine to meet the changing needs of others, just as they will have to adapt to you. A flat refusal to compromise will not benefit you, either in your job or when interacting with friends.

As someone with AS, you may feel there are certain things you have to do on any given day. Although I cannot advise on your specific circumstances, perhaps the following might provide some perspective. On an average day there are only five to six things you 'have' to do to stay healthy:

- eat and drink

- sleep

- visit the toilet

- keep yourself clean

- earn some money

- take medicine (if you are sick).

Virtually everything else you do will be a matter of personal choice and you have a great deal of latitude as to when and how you do those six things. Examine your daily routine against those six things and you may find you have more scope to adapt than you thought.

A sudden change in routine need not be a negative and may lead to a beneficial new experience or opportunity for growth. If thought through, a routine can usually be adapted with minimal disruption. Being occasionally able to 'expect the unexpected' can therefore be a beneficial life skill.

POSITIVE THINKING
Can be hard! I know as someone who can be very negative and who struggles to see the best in any situation. However, the ability to

think positively is essential to combating stress and maintaining good mental health. We all have an endless stream of thoughts running through our head every day. This is known as 'self-talk', and such automatic thoughts can be positive or negative. Some self-talk comes from logic and reason. Other self-talk may arise from misconceptions which are created because of lack of information.

If the thoughts that run through your head are mostly negative, your outlook on life is more likely pessimistic. If your thoughts are mostly positive, you're likely an optimist – someone who practises positive thinking.

There are innumerable self-help books which deal with positive thinking (including this one) and I am not going to repeat their advice, but rather share some insights that have helped me 'stay positive'.

The first is that people (both with and without AS) are not normally good at objectively reviewing their own lives, their own successes and failures, etc. I certainly am not and it seems a cast iron rule that whatever I have been worrying about most is never as serious as it first appears. If you look back at what you have worried about in the past, I am sure you will have had a similar experience. Although this may mean that there is something else I should have been worrying about more, I still find it oddly comforting. If I find myself worrying about something excessively, I am able to console myself by saying that the situation will almost certainly not be as bad as I fear. I am then able to look back on all the occasions when this was true, as evidence of this.

Linked to this is the importance of having someone to talk to. If you are like me, you will frequently have worried over a minor issue until it seems like a major problem. The best way to get that problem back into perspective is to talk about it with someone else. Describing the problem out loud forces you to think more logically about the issue – what the problem is, what the likely impacts will be and what is 'the worst that can happen'. The person you talk to may depend on the problem in question. It may be you need practical help to provide a specific solution, so talking to your boss or another professional (maybe a doctor or counsellor) would be helpful. However, it is sometimes more beneficial to talk to someone with no experience of your problem. This forces you to describe the problem in detail, and think realistically about what is wrong. A more objective opinion (i.e. from a friend, partner or loved one) may provide solutions you would not otherwise have thought of and you may feel more confident about describing the concern to someone who is less likely to judge you.

You should avoid personalising everything and taking responsibility for everything that goes wrong. Try to recognise the role of other factors and people when things go wrong, and remember that sometimes in life things just go wrong and nobody is to blame.

Also, avoid 'hot-button' topics. Maybe you have strong feelings on religious or political issues, but if debating those topics makes you upset or angry then is it really worth it? Remember, you are unlikely to solve the Middle East crisis over a Friday night drink, but you may generate unnecessary stress or anxiety for yourself. If you repeatedly argue about the same subject with the same people, stop bringing it up, or excuse yourself when it's the topic of discussion.

Those with AS generally take life very seriously. It's understandable as generally there is little to find funny in our condition. It makes you sensitive to criticism yet ensures you make innumerable small errors which others feel a constant need to comment upon. Yet that doesn't mean you can't have a sense of humour about life. A sense of humour helps overcome worry by distracting the mind. Laughter may also produce endorphins, which help ease pain and offer a sense of relaxation and joy.

I can't know what you will find funny, but I can say this – if you are something of an outsider in your work or social lives then you are well placed to see just how ridiculous the behaviour of so called 'ordinary' people can be. Perhaps, like me, you've struggled to keep a straight face as two intelligent, adult males talk earnestly for 15 minutes about the ability/inability of a grossly overpaid individual to kick a plastic ball between two metal goalposts. There's a lot to laugh at in the world, if you approach life with a positive frame of mind.

Finally, consider what is really important to you. Society has certain expectations of people – that they should have a successful career, successful love life, a strong group of friends, their own home, etc. However, just because other people want something does not mean that you should automatically want that thing. For example, although I have only had a small number of romantic encounters in my life, this has generally not bothered me. I am usually quite happy on my own and have never felt a romantic relationship to be important. Therefore if you feel that you are failing to achieve something, and that is causing you stress, be sure that the 'something' is what you want, not just something you have been told to want.

GET OUT OF THE HOUSE

My worst periods of stress and anxiety have occurred not at work or in social situations (when my mind has been well occupied) but at home afterwards. Generally, if I have a stressful week followed by a quiet weekend by myself, my stress and anxiety will build up as I brood over my failures (both real and imagined). It is therefore important to have an activity that can take you away from your problems, if only for a while. In my case I regularly go hill walking, and find the country air and great scenery (as well as the mental activity of navigating/map reading) an excellent way to relax.

KNOW YOUR STRENGTHS AND WEAKNESSES

As I discussed, people are not generally very good at objectively judging themselves. Confident people may overstate their strengths; anxious people may overstate their weaknesses and the negative outcomes of any situation. It is important therefore to try and build up a realistic picture of your strengths and weaknesses, both to help you understand where your real problems may be, but also to help build up your confidence in places where you are doing well. There are several ways in which you might do this:

- *Life experience*: Over time your personal successes and failures will show where your general strengths and weaknesses lie. However it is important not to dwell on failures, remember that everyone else will have their own list of success and failures that will be just as long as yours.

- *Objective appraisal*: In something practical, like your job, it is normally fine to ask your boss 'How am I doing?' and if your boss is any good, he should be willing to give constructive feedback. A good appraisal will help reduce any unrealistic concerns, help boost confidence, and identify any areas where improvement is needed.

- *Peer observation:* Your successes and failures are your own. However, occasionally it is beneficial to compare yourself to another person, but only if that person's experiences, position, etc. are comparable to your own. For example, I started my job on the same day as another person and we are therefore at the same place in our career development. Talking to that person, seeing their concerns and frustrations with their job have helped me gain some perspective. Generally, that person gets the same criticisms and praises that I do, and this helps me to see that I am not falling behind or doing worse than I should be at this stage.

ACCEPT THE THINGS YOU CAN'T CHANGE

Some sources of stress are unavoidable. As someone with AS and dyslexia, I have to accept that I will make a whole range of mistakes that others won't, and I probably always will. In such cases, the best way to cope with stress is to accept things as they are. Acceptance may be difficult, but in the long run it's easier than railing against a situation you can't change. Remember that many things in life are beyond our control – particularly the behaviour of other people. Rather than stressing out over them, focus on the things you can control, such as the way you choose to react to problems.

The most important thing is to learn to forgive – both yourself and others. Throughout your life, you will get innumerable comments, criticisms, judgements, and unwanted 'advice' from those who mean well (and those who don't), and you to will doubtless give plenty of offence to others. However, no one will be harder on you than yourself, as you look back over past mistakes. Sooner or later you will have to accept the fact that we live in an imperfect world and that people (including you) make mistakes. Time is a great healer and the sooner you can 'forgive and forget' the sooner you can get on with your life.

Contributors

8ball works in the pharmaceutical industry. That isn't code for is a petty drug dealer, by the way. He does stuff with computers for them, database stuff, which is apparently quite a normal thing for an Aspie to be doing. In his spare time he is slightly afraid of dogs and horses.

Debbie Allan is known as Debs to her family. Her hobbies are caring for animals and anything involving arts and crafts. She also likes going for walks and meeting friends for coffee. She is really interested in genealogy and has found out a lot of information about her ancestors. She keeps fit by swimming a few times a week. Since being diagnosed with Asperger syndrome at the age of 44 Debbie's life has changed a great deal. She is now less critical and more accepting of herself than she previously was and understands now why she found some of her jobs so difficult. She has also made new friends with other people with Asperger syndrome.

Luke Beardon, Senior Lecturer in Autism, has worked in the field of autism for many years in a range of capacities. He currently works at The Autism Centre, Sheffield Hallam University, where he supports people with autism, families, and professionals, as well as lecturing and providing consultancy.

E. Veronica Bliss (Vicky) recognizes many indicators of Asperger syndrome in her own personal history, but the condition for her is as yet undiagnosed. She has worked for over 20 years with people who have autism as well as people with other differences and has worked as a solution-focused psychologist for many years.

Alex Brown lives in North Yorkshire with her husband David, three cats and a Chilean Rose Tarantula called Horace. Alex has worked full-time within library services, mainly in an administrative role, since August 2001. Alex was diagnosed with AS in 2007 aged 38. Her greatest achievement in life is her daughter, who has recently left home to attend university. Her favourite places include woodlands, the countryside and the seashore.

Janet Christmas was born in Hull in 1955 and educated in Lincolnshire and boarding school in Norfolk. She qualified as a geologist by reading for a BSc in Geology at University College of Wales, Swansea followed by an MSc at Sheffield University. Following a five-year career as a geologist on oil rigs in the North Sea, she moved to London and worked as a civil servant from 1987 to 2004. Currently living in Norfolk with her mother, Janet has two part-time jobs locally in retail. She regularly contributes to online discussion groups on the topic of Asperger syndrome.

Cornish received his diagnosis at the age of 44 in 2003. Since then he has become a qualified consultant in Asperger syndrome. Cornish is a co Director of the Adult Asperger Consultancy set up in 2010, which caters for adults, family and carer's, and covers all aspects of support. Cornish also lectures on the Under and Post grad courses run through Sheffield Hallam, and is a nationwide speaker and presenter, and expert in all things Aspergian.

Natasha Goldthorpe has just completed her postgraduate certificate in Asperger syndrome and currently works with adults and teenagers with Asperger syndrome. Asperger syndrome remains a long standing interest and, in particular, how it presents in females; a topic Natasha explores through personal projects such as producing a radio documentary. Natasha lives with her partner, with whom she is expecting her first child, and loves to travel abroad, walk her Cocker Spaniel Piper, write, sing and organise events.

Anne Henderson has a son with Asperger syndrome who has turned his life around after a very difficult start. He is working towards supported living after a period in hospital and then residential care. He has learnt to overcome some of his difficulties with the excellent, consistent care and support provided. He is employed on a part-time and voluntary basis in the provider's Head Office, does voluntary work in a charity shop and on a conservation project. This has been achieved by his own hard work and the outstanding contribution from his care provider, willing to work together – he is now leading a busy, happy life.

Steve Jarvis was diagnosed with Asperger syndrome in 2005 at the age of 45. Finally having an explanation for difficulties in his life has made a big difference to his mental health. He works as a learning consultant and lives alone in Hertfordshire. He enjoys singing bass in a local a cappella choir and spending time with his friends. He knows he is fortunate to have been able to hold down a job all his adult life and this has also been crucial to his mental health.

Wendy Lim had a late diagnosis of Asperger syndrome at the age of 42. She has a teenage son and also has three grown up sons. Whilst there's a lot of emphasis on supporting the parents of children with AS, Wendy would like to see more recognition that some Aspies are parents and carers themselves. She suffers from social phobia and selective mutism and so continues to really struggle socially. Wendy has spent some time learning how to make jewellery and is now beginning to design and sell her own handmade jewellery. She has also recently started doing some 'behind the scenes' voluntary work in a small hostel that is near her home.

Lynette Marshall is proud to have AS. She has developed some very good friendships with some fantastic people and gained the confidence to seek a diagnosis in 2008. Her life is dedicated to supporting children and young people with autism. Currently in her final year of a Masters in autism, Lynette is looking forward to graduating again in the summer. With thanks to Luke Beardon who made it all possible. Luke – you cannot be thanked enough.

Chris Mitchell was diagnosed with Asperger syndrome in 1998 when he was 20 years old before graduating from the University of Northumbria with an MA (Hons) in Information and Library Management in 2001. Chris has published two books, *Glass Half-Empty Glass Half Full: How Asperger's Syndrome Changed My Life* and *Asperger's Syndrome and Mindfulness: Taking Refuge in the Buddha*. He is also an active advocate for Asperger syndrome, giving talks, seminars and workshops throughout the UK and internationally. In 2010, he was appointed to the position of Operations Manager at Autism Works, a social enterprise that employs people on the autistic spectrum in software testing.

Anthony Sclafani is a 33-year-old male from the United States and was diagnosed with Asperger syndrome back in November 2001. Currently Anthony works full time in a Registrar's Office at a community college. His diagnosis of Asperger syndrome has enabled him to understand more about himself after many years of not knowing the reason of his differences.

Neil Shepherd was diagnosed with Asperger syndrome when he was 31 after struggling for years to hold down a job in the IT industry, remain sane and do all of the things that 'normal' people do. Married, divorced, and survivor of suicide attempts, domestic abuse and workplace bullying, he has written two books on the subject of growing up and living with AS (*Wired-Up Wrong* and *Wired-Up Right*, both published by lulu.com) and has contributed to several other books on the subject.

Melanie Smith found that until she was 12 years old, it was a hard battle for professionals to recognise that she was under the autistic spectrum. After years of trying to get diagnosed she was finally able to attend a special school that catered to her needs and specialised in autism spectrum differences. Throughout that time, Melanie gained enough qualifications such as GCSEs and finally A-levels to allow her to attend college and she has just recently completed her first year of university studying psychology. This is a huge achievement for her as she struggled with academic ability until she was finally taught properly.

Dr Christopher Wilson is a Regeneration Consultant with the Warrington based consultancy firm, BE Group. He completed his doctorate at Manchester University in 2006, researching community involvement in local housing improvement programmes. Christopher was diagnosed with dyslexia in childhood and also has a likely (but not confirmed) diagnosis of Asperger syndrome. He regularly engages with the Asperger's support website 'Aspie Village' and participates in Aspie Village events and meet-ups.

Dean Worton was diagnosed age 28 and finally had an answer for many of his mysterious problems. For the last few years he has been a local authority technical support officer, which he enjoys. He spends much of his spare time running an internet support group for UK based adults with Asperger syndrome and arranging meetings for its members, as well as often helping out with other projects to help other people with AS. Dean has a positive outlook on life and makes the best he can out of it.